CUTTING

D0528653

BLOCK PLANE

These pocket-size planes are perfect for smaller jobs, fitting jobs in finish carpentry, and furniture making. Block planes were specifically developed to cut end grain. These are just great little tools to own.

A standard block plane is often used as a one-handed cutting tool, and while it's too small to straighten boards, it is unsurpassed in making small adjustments to miters, or removing saw blade marks from the edge of a board that has been ripped to width.

The block plane is engineered to cut with the grain, but it was conceived as a cross-grain cutting tool. The typical block plane's blade is set low at 21 degrees and makes a shallow cut, thus lowering the chance of tear-out. Tear-out is nothing more than a splintery cut made in wood. Low-angle block planes have the blade set at about 12 degrees, and when properly sharpened, will cut translucent ribbons of wood for amazingly precise results in furniture making, finish carpentry, and boat building. If you have to remember one thing about these planes, it's this: unlike a larger bench plane, which operates with the cutter's bevel facing down, the bevel on a block plane's cutter faces up.

PLANE AND SIMPLE *These handy tools are bursting with life lessons: remove a little stock at a time; feel the tool through the work; sharp tools work best; and more. Stanley's 12-220 is a mainstay. Scope out Lee Valley or Bridge City for higher-end items. And remember, woodworkers always lay planes on their side when they're not using them—to protect the iron's edge.*

BOW SAW

The bow saw is a pruning tool for cutting branches that are less than 10 inches in diameter. The saw makes quick work of getting through a branch because the ribbon-thin blade has an aggressive set of teeth. Based on a design by the Sandvik Company out of Sweden in the 1950s, these tough, lightweight, and inexpensive saws cut quickly. They are the tool of choice for many landscapers and homeowners, as well as hunters who need to make a duck blind or clear small branches for a tree stand.

Pruning a branch takes a bit of know-how. To prune a good-sized branch, you must first undercut it about 6 to 12 inches from the trunk. This cut, a relief cut really, should only go $1/4$ to $1/3$ of the way through the branch. Then, start the top cut about 2 inches past the undercut, away from the trunk. Depending on the size of the branch, it may snap off before you've completed your through cut. Don't worry if you've got a ragged, jagged, or fractured branch on your hands. You've got a sizable stub that you can easily and neatly cut. Don't cut too close to the trunk though. On most trees, there's a little swell around the branch where it meets the trunk, as if the branch were coming out of a sleeve. That's called the branch collar. Make your final cut just beyond the branch collar to ensure the tree's health.

While a bow saw is safer than a chain saw for removing tree limbs while standing on a ladder, it's not the tool to use if you've got some trees to drop or storm damage to clean up. For those kinds of jobs, a chain saw is your best friend.

2

CHAIN SAW

You have two choices on powering this irreplaceable logging tool. If you've got smaller jobs close to home, an electric saw might be your best choice. An electric version is lighter than its gas-powered counterpart, quieter, and cleaner. There's a tradeoff, though. It's not nearly as powerful, and it's simply not suited for heavy work, because it's tethered to an exterior outlet by an extension cord.

Select a gas chain saw for most jobs. A saw with an engine in the 30- to 40-cc range with an 18-inch bar is perfect for cutting up winter-damaged storm limbs and landscape maintenance work, and it will do just fine for preparing small amounts of firewood. For heavy cutting, you'll need a saw in the 55- to 60-cc range, equipped with a bar from 18 to 22 inches.

Most importantly, don't skimp on the safety gear. Get protective earmuffs, chaps, leather work gloves, and wraparound eye protection.

Other tools and accessories that can make woodcutting more productive and safer are felling wedges (pounded into a felling cut, they push a tree over), log hooks, and two-person timber carriers. Also consider a traditional logging tool: the cant hook or the pointed version of that tool, the peavey. Both are extremely useful for turning and positioning difficult logs. We vote thumbs down on one logging tool: the steel saw buck, which is obviously a disaster if you hit it with a saw chain. Instead, build your own saw buck out of pressure-treated lumber. Hit that with the chain, and it's no big deal.

CIRCULAR SAW

With amperage ratings between 13 and 15 amps and armed with a 7 ¹/₄-inch blade, there's not much these saws can't cut. Lock in a masonry blade, and these saws will scream through concrete (this kicks up a ton of fine dust, so wear a respirator). With the right blades, you can knock through composite materials, plywood, and dimensional lumber in no time flat.

Aside from the importance of amperage (which correlates directly to the saw's power) and weight (which correlates directly to user fatigue), you want your saw to be a real fit for you. Before buying one, hold the saw and get a sense of it. Make sure it will fit your gloved hand. Other things you'll want to check are blade depth and bevel adjustments. You'll want easy-to-read adjustment scales and easy-to-reach levers.

Circular saws span a great range of models. The most popular is the sidewinder circular saw, which features good durability, light weight, and is easy to use. Need more torque and toughness? Try a worm-drive circular saw. If maneuverability for cutting sheet goods, siding, and flooring is paramount, we suggest the light 4 ¹/₂-inch-bladed trim saw.

A fourth model is a track saw, which is the saw of choice for many scrupulous cabinetmakers and finish carpenters. These saws come with a proprietary track system, allowing you to make rips and cuts with the accuracy of a table saw, but with one advantage: portability and ease. It's far easier to push a 12-pound saw through a 95-pound sheet of medium-density fiberboard than it is to balance and push that same sheet across a table saw. If space is an issue, or just the bulk and weight of a table saw has you stalemated, a track saw is a great alternative.

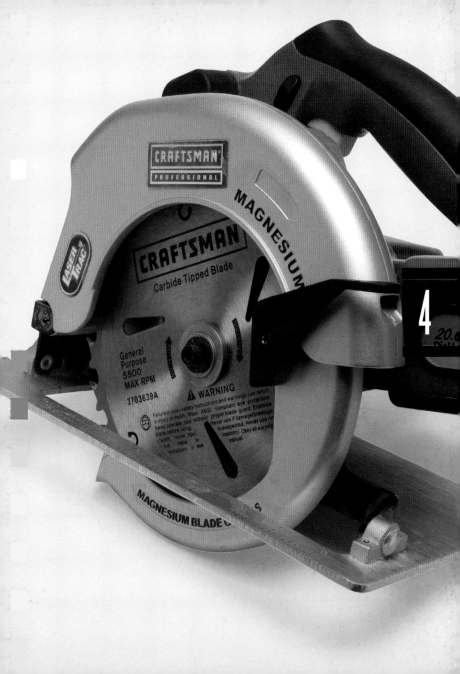

COLD CHISEL

Use a cold chisel to chop through bolts, rivets, and pins, and to cut cold (as opposed to torch- or forge-heated) metal. Strike it with a ball-peen hammer, preferably one with a head $1/8$ inch larger than the end of the chisel. You can get a better view of the tip by gripping the body with tongue-and-groove pliers. Always wear safety glasses when striking a cold chisel, and never use it on stone or concrete.

Some of these tools are now equipped with a polymer cap, which does two things. First, it reduces the "mushrooming head" and the risk of flying metal fragments during impact. Second, the polymer cap forms a larger striking surface than the chisel itself, and that protects your hand as you hold the chisel.

A cold chisel is generally used to remove waste metal when a smooth finish isn't required. Because these tools are used to cut metal, they have a less acute cutting angle than a typical wood chisel. This gives the tool a less sharp, but stronger, cutting edge.

SPECIALIZED CUTS *While the flat chisel is a must for your toolbox, you may need a variety of sizes on standby for different projects. We recommend picking up a three- or five-piece set containing a mix of sizes, including a ¼-inch and a ¾-inch. And one more tip: We suggest slipping a plastic safety sleeve over the chisel to protect your hand from a misplaced blow with a hammer. Some chisels, such as Stanley's FatMax series, come with this installed.*

5

COPING SAW

This exacting and inexpensive saw is a gem for making intricate cuts. Taking its name from the function it provides, coping, it is the preferred method for making the inside corners of moldings look good.

The saw is designed to cut on the pull stroke, but many people set the blade to cut on the push stroke. Depending what you're cutting, there is an assortment of blades available, but most people make do with a blade with 15 teeth per inch. Fewer teeth makes for faster sawing but a rougher cut. More teeth means a smoother cut.

The first step in coping a piece of molding is to establish your cut line. With a miter saw, cut the molding at a 45-degree angle. Make a pencil mark highlighting the molding's profile. Then, back cut the piece of molding to create a mirror image of the abutting profile. It takes some practice, but when done right, your cut will mate neatly with another piece of molding like an interlocking puzzle piece.

Hold or clamp the molding down on a bench or saw horse and ease the blade into the wood. Don't force it. If the blade wanders away from your cut line, back it out and start again. Chances are you won't make the cut in a single run—especially with complex molding profiles. You'll probably have to ease your cut with 100-grit sandpaper or a file for a perfect fit.

6

CROSSCUT SAW

Even if you own an arsenal of power saws, an eight-point crosscut saw should have a place of honor in your shop. It may not make the finest cut, but it's the perfect jack-of-all-trades saw for small jobs, like that occasional 2 x 4.

To make a cut, mark your line and cut to the waste side. Start your cut by drawing the saw lightly backward while holding it at a shallow angle to get the blade started. Use the thumb of your hand that's holding the board as a guide, and hold the saw so its toothed edge is approximately 45 degrees to the work surface. Push the saw forward using full strokes and as much of the blade as possible. You're cutting with the push stroke, so don't bear down on the saw; it'll just slow you down. Let the saw cut the wood. Your job is to move the saw back and forth.

As you complete the cut, lower the angle of the saw to minimize splintering the cut on the board's bottom. Make sure the final draw is a slow backwards pull. And one more tip: if the kerf closes on the blade, jamming you up, slip a 16d common nail into the kerf to hold it open.

A CUT ABOVE *If you're looking for the perfect pegboard centerpiece, we recommend either Lee Valley's Wenzloff Cross-cut Panel Saw or Thomas Flinn's PAX Panel Saw. Neither are cheap, but their classic design, hand-sharpened spring-steel blades, wood handles, and taper-ground precision will make you wonder why you didn't upgrade earlier.*

7

DRILL BIT

For general hole drilling, a set of fifteen or eighteen high-speed steel twist drill bits will suffice. These bits work great on wood and most plastics.

Titanium nitride–coated bits are a better choice for industrial use or drilling truly abrasive materials, like cast iron. The titanium nitride coating over the high-speed steel improves the bit's abrasion resistance, helping it hold an edge longer. Expensive specialty bits like concrete bits, auger bits, and countersinks come in handy as well. We suggest buying these bits individually, as the need arises, instead of an entire set.

And make sure you're using the right drill bit. Spade bits cut aggressively and are designed for quick, rough holes. Screw point auger bits pull themselves through the wood and bore with high speed, leaving a relatively rough exit hole. Hollow center auger bits are aggressive enough to cut right through nails and will chug through green, wet wood. Brad point twist bits bore with high speed and precision, leaving a clean exit hole. Finally, Forstner bits cut large diameter holes (up to 4 in. across). These larger diameter bits are intended to be used in a drill press.

WHERE'S THE POINT? *Heat and friction rob our bits of a honed edge just as dropping them or hitting a nail will. But don't toss your dull bits; sharpen them using a Drill Doctor. This handy accessory will help you keep your bits sharper than on the day you bought them, and using it is as easy as sharpening a pencil. The budget model (DD350X) is great for hobbyists, but if you're looking to resurrect those custom, carbide-tipped masonry bits, you'll need the DD750X.*

DRYWALL SAW

A drywall saw, or jab saw, is used for cutting holes for outlets and switches or when used carefully, making a reasonably accurate hole for a recessed light. These dagger-like handsaws offer the perfect approach. After precisely transferring your measurements onto your drywall (for recessed lights, use a compass like the one you had as a kid to make the circles), push the tip of this saw through the drywall. Some tips are pretty dull but can be ground to a sharper point so that jabbing them through the drywall will be relatively clean.

The aggressive tooth is designed to cut on both the push and pull strokes. The handles are either wood, plastic, or rubberized. They all work, but if you plan on using this saw day in and day out, you might opt for a more-cushioned rubberized handle. When cutting drywall where you have access to both sides of its surface, stay to the good side of the sheet. By "good side" we mean the side that will face into the room. When you cut, it's a good idea to back cut the opening. In other words, cut on an angle so the back of the cut is a bit wider than the front. This gives you a little oops room without affecting the face of the drywall.

Not all jab saws are created equal. Many manufacturers make saws that are great on standard drywall but will simply not cut cement board or dense fire-rated drywall. Search out specific makes that the manufacturers rate for these materials.

9

HACKSAW

The fine-tooth blade of a hacksaw can cut through iron and steel as well as through tough materials like hard plastics and cable. With a blade known as a carbide-grit rod saw, it can even slice through ceramic tile. For metal, use a carbon-steel blade with 14, 18, 24, or 32 teeth per inch. Opt for a bimetal blade for high-tension pro models, which exert tremendous tensile force to hold the blade arrow straight in tough cuts. The bimetal blade's carbon-steel back bonded to a high-speed-steel front can take the tension.

A hacksaw frame can be fixed or adjustable. An adjustable frame gives you some room to pick blades from 8 to 16 inches in length. In addition to the adjustable frames, the posts that hold the blades can be set in different positions, so you can cut left, right, up, or down.

When installing the blade, the teeth should be pointing forward, or away from the handle. Your cut time should be one second per stroke. Use the length of the blade when possible, so take it slow. Since you create a great deal of heat when using a hacksaw, a drop or two of clear cutting oil will help reduce the heat and keep your blade sharp for a longer time.

BLADES OF GLORY *A hacksaw is perfect to saw off those large bolts, stuck screws, and broken hardware, but sometimes there's just no room to manuever. We suggest combining the best of two worlds: grip a hacksaw blade in a pair of locking pliers. And for those really confining spaces, use a snapped-off piece of hacksaw blade.*

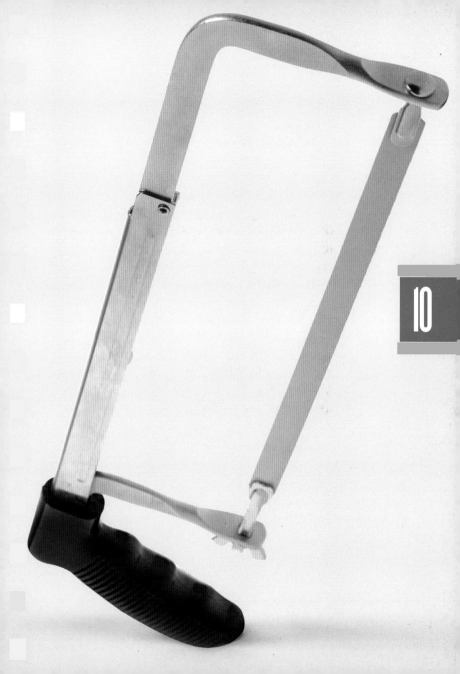

JIGSAW

The real bread-and-butter use for a jigsaw is cutting freehand curves in wood, metal, or plastic. Achieving these graceful curves, semicircles, or arcs takes some practice. While we advise cutting wide of your line and then sanding, filing, or planing your material into its final shape, having the right blade makes a big difference. Thin blades with a higher tpi (teeth per inch) are the most maneuverable and cleanest-cutting blades. A thick blade with fewer teeth is for roughing a shape close to where you want it.

Cutting freehand circles with a jigsaw is tough to get right, but using a trammel is an excellent way to cut spot-on curves and circles. For smaller circles though, nothing beats a good hole saw on your cordless drill.

And there's more this saw can do. Another cool function is coping crown molding. The Collins coping foot is an aftermarket base that fits most jigsaws and turns them into power coping saws. Like any other skill, coping takes some practice to get it just right.

Not every saw performs equally, so make sure to consider the features available before purchasing this little tool, which include hands-free blade changing, blade guides (to keep the blade cutting square to the base), and splinter guards to minimize tear-out.

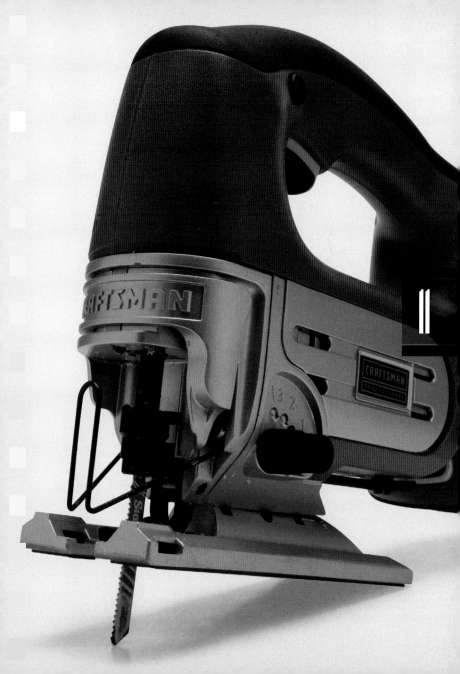

MITER SAW

A miter saw is also called a chop saw because the blade comes down into the workpiece like a karate chop. It is a portable, precision instrument that every trim carpenter or woodworker must own. Which saw is right for you depends on what you're going to do. If you plan on cutting wide crown, baseboard, 2 x 10s, or 4x stock, then a 12-inch sliding compound miter saw is the right tool for you.

But if you're using it mostly for smaller stock, a minisliding compound miter saw may be exactly what you need, featuring a 7 1/4-inch blade has an 11 3/4-inch crosscut capacity and the ability to cut a 2 x 8 at 45 degrees. While this saw will not cut through 4x stock or wide crown moldings, it is much lighter than the 10-or 12-inch models.

Direct-drive miter saws have the motor in line with the blade and are the least expensive saws available. But with a direct-drive saw, the motor's vibrations transfer directly to the blade and may cost you some precision in your cuts. Direct-drive saws are perfect for plumbing, flooring, and landscaping work.

With a belt-driven saw, the blade isn't affected by the motor's vibration, and these saws offer a consistent cutting depth on either side of the blade. The motor sits back out of the way and lets you make a compound miter on either side of the blade. A belt-driven saw is preferred for making furniture, built-ins, and fireplace mantles, and for other finish carpentry tasks where precision is a must.

And one more thing: buy or make a stand for this saw. Crawling around on the floor trying to eye a careful miter is no way to work.

PIPE AND TUBING CUTTER

When it comes to running copper pipe for plumbing applications or copper tubing for gas lines—or any other thin-walled metal tube, whether it's brass, copper, aluminum, or conduit—a hacksaw should stay put; reach for a better tool.

Tubing cutters are compact, require virtually no swing room, and can accommodate tubing with an outside diameter (OD) from 1/8 inch to 1 1/8 inches. Simply set the tube into the jaws and turn the knurled knob that raises the cutting wheel until it's finger tight. Once the cutting wheel has made contact, turn the tool a full turn around the tubing, scoring it. With each revolution, you'll raise the cutting wheel just a bit, and after two or three revolutions, the cut will be complete. The result is a superclean perpendicular cut that provides the strongest, most secure joints when making soldered connections.

Ream off the small burr on the inside of the cut surface, and you're ready to begin solder preparations for plumbing jobs or to fit up with conduit body and connectors for electrical work.

PLASTIC ABOUT THAT *Working with copper tubing or plastic? Or perhaps it's cast iron and concrete? Believe us when we say there's a cutter engineered specifically for every type of piping. For example, pictured is Ridgid's Scissor-Style Cutter, specifically created to swipe through all types of plastic and rubber tubing (up to 1 7/8" outside diameter) in one go—no ratcheting or twisting required. Copper and other metal pipes require a more recognizable design. Match your tool to the job for the cleanest cut: there's a tool developed for close quarters, soil pipes, and much more.*

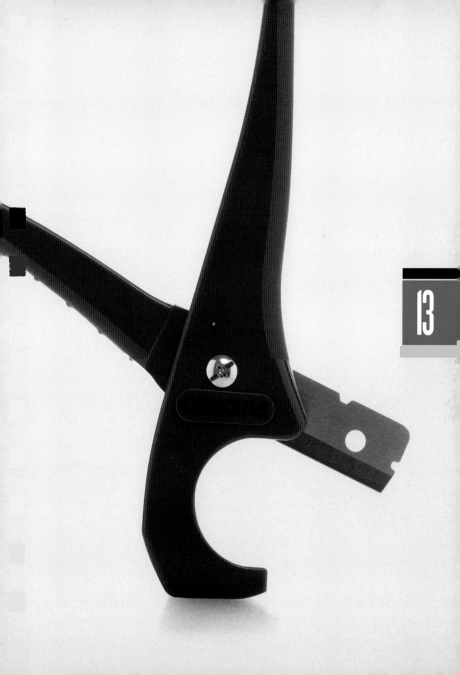

13

RECIPROCATING SAW

The reciprocating saw is one of those indispensable tools that proves its worth the first time you go to install a door or skylight or, for that matter, do nearly any demolition task around the house. It's not a precision instrument, but in the right hands, you might think it is. The saw works like an aggressive electric carving knife. The blade reciprocates at tremendous speed and power. Combine that with blade sizes ranging from a mere 3-inches to 16-inches long, and there isn't anything you can't cut with one of these tools, from a rusty bolt to a piece of lumber to a stubborn tree root. And these blades are designed for specific tasks. There are specific wood-cutting blades, and blades strictly for metal use. Additionally, bimetal blades can cut through wood, metal, and other miscellaneous materials at the same time. There are even diamond-grit blades, which excel at particularly tough jobs, like cutting cast-iron pipe.

A good reciprocating saw will have a double-insulated body to reduce the risk of shocks, even if you cut a live electrical wire (and it happens). Many models have variable speeds, which is a necessity for this kind of tool, since it is used to cut plastic, plaster, metal, wood, asphalt shingles, tree limbs, you name it. Emergency responders, like firefighters and EMT crews, carry these saws to perform many tasks, including extrications.

Electricians, plumbers, and landscapers, who don't use the saw the way a remodeler does, might be well-served with a cordless model. But for those heavy-duty jobs, grab hold of an industrial-quality 15 amp variable-speed saw with an orbital cutting option. It'll tear through just about anything in front of it.

14

ROUTER

Routers are one of the most popular woodworking tools around for making dadoes and dovetails and performing any number of joinery operations, as well as adding a decorative flair to the edge of a surface, such as a shelf or table top.

The first thing to consider when shopping for a router is horsepower. Horsepower determines the work that the machine can do and the diameter of the bits it can handle. General-purpose routers are 1 to 2 horsepower, whereas heavy-duty routers used in cabinet shops usually rate 3 horsepower or better.

The most versatile of these handheld tools is the D-handle router. The D-handle configuration is easy to grab, and the on/off switch is under your index finger, like a trigger. There will be no more fumbling for the toggle switch while the tool in your hand spins at 10,000 rpm.

Typically, the tool will come with ¹/₄-inch and ¹/₂-inch collets. Whenever possible, stick with the ½-inch collets and bits. The ¹/₂-inch bits are eight times stronger than the smaller bits and cut smoother, especially in hardwoods and sheet goods.

The D-handle is the go-to setup for a fixed base. A plunge base lets you do all the things a fixed base does plus lets you alter the depth of the cut on the fly. The plunge base safely lowers the bit into the wood, instead of having to start at the board's edge—perfect for making mortises or decorative columns for your house.

When buying a router, get a kit with at least two of these three bases: a plunge, fixed, and D-handle. It costs a bit more at first, but it gives you the freedom to tackle a number of jobs with one tool.

15

SIDE-CUTTING PLIERS

Call them side cutters, linesman pliers, or electrician's pliers.
By any name, the heavy jaws and shears make this tool indispensable for cutting electrical cable and for pulling the steel tape used to fish wires through wall and ceiling cavities. Models rated as "high leverage" can cut nails and bolts, while those equipped with a die near the jaws can press together the crimp connectors used on grounding wires. It's a multifunctional tool with dexterity to boot.

When cutting with these tools, always make sure you, and anyone around you, are wearing safety glasses. You should never cut hardened wire unless the pliers are specifically engineered for this use. If the knives can't make the cut at a right angle, you need bigger pliers.

And it should go without saying that you should never work on live wires. Those plastic-dipped handles aren't insulated unless they say they are specifically rated as so; that plastic coating is for comfort, not functionality.

CUT TO THE CHASE *Linesman pliers share the name of side cutters with diagonal pliers ("dikes" for short), which has only one function: cutting wire. Linesman pliers cut and grab, and some models (like the one pictured) also strip and crimp. All linesman pliers are side cutters, but not all side cutters are linesman pliers.*

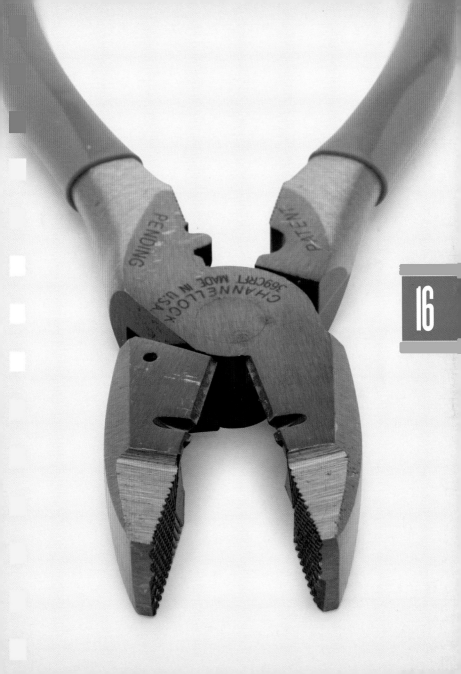

16

SNIPS

You don't have to be a metalworker to appreciate snips. This tool cuts steel, copper, or aluminum sheets and also cuts rubber, heavy cardboard, and plastic. Pro models have color-coded handles to indicate whether they are designed for left curves, right curves, or straight cuts (red, green, and yellow, respectively). Some blades have a serrated edge, which helps you keep a grip on the metal but leaves a more ragged cut than a nonserrated blade. Most homeowners can get by with a single all-purpose utility snip.

Your first time cutting with a pair of snips may be challenging. Snips are not scissors for metal. To make a cut, pull the bottom blade up and keep the top blade lined up with your cut line. For long cuts in sheet metal, use an awl to mark the cut line. Be careful and use a straightedge; don't freehand it. And don't rush it.

When you work with any type of sheet metal, wear a pair of heavy-duty leather gloves. A freshly cut piece of sheet metal is very sharp.

As for a preference on the model of snips to purchase, consider offset aviation snips. The offset blades keep your hands clear of the work, and they offer a more natural cutting position, while giving better leverage to cut thicker material. Also known as compound-action snips, sheet snips, or maille snips, these powerhouses were developed to cut aluminum in aircraft construction and can handle aluminum up to 18 gauge, stainless steel up to 26 gauge, and mild steel up to 24 gauge with ease.

17

UTILITY KNIFE

Utility knives have come a long way since their introduction.
With tool-free access to blade storage in the handle and smooth-sliding retractable blades, newer versions of the tool are easier to use, offer a better grip, and may include other features, such as a slot for slitting string. There are also folding versions of the knife, which work much like a pocket knife. They are easy to stow in a pocket, and many come with a belt clip.

The beauty of the utility knife lies in its simplicity. Like many great tools, it isn't designed for one particular purpose, but instead is absolutely indispensable for tackling dozens of jobs. If you've been using yours only to cut twine and open packages, then you've been missing out. There's a lot this little tool can do: from cutting batts of insulation to making mincemeat of cardboard; trimming wood shims to scribing hinge mortises; opening packages to rescuing paint-coated screws.

It can even sharpen your carpenter's pencils. You'll have to agree it's more than just a handle with a sharp, pointy blade, right?

A RAZOR'S EDGE *Utility knives with minimal bells and whistles won't break the bank, running between $5 and $15. So why not spring for the best out there? Find a knife that feels comfortable in your grip—and easy-access blade storage, so you'll never have to scrounge for a replacement. Take a look at Stanley and Craftsman for dependable models.*

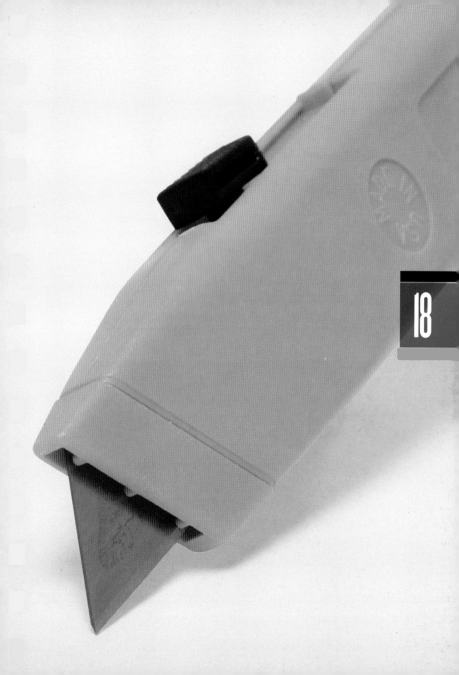

WOOD CHISEL

For proper cutting, the back of the wood chisel must be perfectly flat and the beveled edge has to be sharp. Using a chisel is not difficult, and with a little practice, you'll be mortising hinges or repairing damaged trim details like a pro.

To mortise a hinge, trace the hinge onto the door or jamb. With the chisel, score the outline, making sure to keep the beveled face of the chisel toward the mortise. You'll only want to score to the depth of the hinge. Once the outline is finished, make a series of shallow cuts across the grain about every quarter of an inch or so. Gently tap the chisel and be aware of your depth as you cut. Once you've made your crosscuts, take out the wood between them using the chisel bevel side down. Finish paring the bottom of the mortise flat with the bevel side up.

Some wood chisels have a metal shaft, or tang, that runs from the large steel striking cap all the way to the blade. This makes for a stronger chisel, and when you strike it with a hammer, very little of the force gets absorbed by the handle. This type of chisel is a stronger tool and can be used for the most rugged chopping in carpentry, furniture construction, and building boats.

When you're looking for your set, we recommend picking up at least four: a ¼", ½", ¾" and 1". These four chisels will last you a lifetime if cared for properly. To hone a chisel, work the bevel over a sharpening stone so that you form a burr on its tip (known as the wire edge). Flip it over then hone the back, removing the wire edge in the process. One or two more strokes on the bevel, then one or two on the back, and you're done.

19

TIGHTENING

ADJUSTABLE WRENCH

Solymon Merrick is credited with the patent on the adjustable wrench in 1835, and as the tool's name implies, it can fit a variety of sized nuts or bolts. The jaw opens by turning a wheel at the head and is good for British Standard Whitworth as well as metric-sized fasteners. If you're going to own just one, make it a 10- or 14-inch model so that it's big enough for residential plumbing fittings. They do range in size from the ultra-portable 4-inch, which is great for cyclists to make roadside bike repairs, to the industrial-sized 24-inch.

Whether you're tightening or loosening a fastener, be sure the fixed jaw, not the moveable part, is applying the force. Position yourself so you are pulling the wrench, not pushing it. Pushing it raises the risk of having the wrench slip. If you do apply force to the moveable jaw, there's a chance that it might move and slip off the bolt, possibly banging up your knuckles and rounding the edges of your fastener, which will make it very difficult to tighten or loosen it further.

Many mechanics will recommend using an adjustable wrench only for plumbing. There's too much movement in the jaws, often called slop, which creates a knuckle-buster waiting to happen, and they would recommend a good set of fixed wrenches instead. But for a quick job, or just to lighten your toolbox, an adjustable wrench is just the right tool most of the time.

20

ALLEN WRENCH

Also known as hex wrenches or hex keys, Allen wrenches have a hexagonal cross section to fit screw heads with hexagonal recesses, common in bicycles, motorcycle engines and, increasingly, build-it-yourself furniture. With motorcycles, Allen fastener heads allow an engine cover to be mounted flush to an engine case without protruding bolt heads. Unlike the Phillips heads briefly used in mid-'80s Japanese bikes, the Allen bolts can actually be removed—as long as you have the right size for the job.

Allen wrenches are made in fractional inch and metric sizes. The three most common sizes are $^5/_{32}$ inch, $^3/_{16}$ inch, and $^1/_4$ inch; in metric, 4, 5, and 6 millimeters see a lot of action. Other good SAE sizes to own are $^3/_{32}$ inch, $^7/_{64}$ inch, $^1/_8$ inch, $^9/_{64}$ inch, and $^7/_{32}$ inch. It's difficult to say what sizes are common when assembling furniture, because as anyone with experience at that job knows, those little L-shaped keys tend to disappear immediately.

This is why storage is critical. Keeping the tools together on a ring is a good start. But as long as you're working with an L-shaped tool shorter than a broken pencil, you're always going to have a little stub of metal gouging your palm with each torque. The better bet is to find a tool with some actual thought put into its design.

Some options include the traditional fold-up style, in which the wrenches pull out like pocketknives from a nicely sized handle; or the more unusual three-way wrenches, which arrange common sizes on an easy-to-grip disk shaped like a Chinese throwing star. If you really want to get fancy (and save serious time and effort), consider investing in Garrett Wade's ratcheting Allen wrench.

GREENLEE®

21

COMBINATION WRENCH

Your wife has the family silver tucked away in a felt-lined box, but you've got your set of combination wrenches. The tool's design is prototypically simple—box-end on one side, open on the other. It has no moving parts and is covered in shiny chrome. If you're lucky enough to have inherited the set from your dad, that makes it as precious as the silver, though cheaper to insure.

No one knows who invented the combination wrench or when, but it was popularized in the United States by Plomb Tools in the 1930s, a period of social and technological ferment. As automobiles became more numerous and sophisticated, so did the tools to work on them. New steel alloys and forging methods have only improved the wrench with the passage of time.

Today's wrench is thinner, sleeker, and stronger than the bulky ones it replaces; it weighs half what it did in the '20s. While it is hard to improve on perfection, in 2006 Craftsman introduced a new twist—literally—in its Cross-Force combination wrenches, turning the handle so your palm presses on the tool's broad face, not the narrow edge.

You can purchase sets in a variety of assortments, but whatever set you purchase should include at least these seven sizes: $3/8$", $7/16$", $1/2$", $9/16$", $5/8$", $11/16$", and $3/4$". And if you'll be working on anything outside the U.S., add five metric wrenches, from 10mm to 14mm.

Back when blacksmiths forged tools, they would inscribe the year on the head, as if to announce that it would last decades, maybe centuries, into an uncertain future. A fine set of wrenches, bearing dates or not, exudes the same sense of permanence.

IMPACT DRIVER

If you're still using a drill to drive screws, you don't know what you're missing. An impact driver operates with about 1,400 inch-pounds of torque—triple what a drill/driver puts out—without delivering that torque to the handle of the tool, like a cordless drill will. That alone saves your wrist from some serious next-day aching.

Impact drivers are designed to do one thing well, and that's drive screws. Drill/drivers, on the other hand, are effective screwdrivers, but their effectiveness drops off with larger fasteners, especially really big ones, like lag screws. Impact drivers combine rotation with concussive blows to improve their screwdriving capability, especially when sinking a fastener in tough material, like pressure-treated lumber.

Right now, lithium-ion-powered tools rule the roost. They are much lighter, and the batteries charge faster and hold their charge longer than NiCad or NiMH batteries do. Something to consider when buying one of these tools is if it comes equipped with a light (most do). While that may seem hokey, wait till you're in a dark attic putting in some duct work or you're working under a deck. Then it becomes a blessing. The other thing you'll want, aside from a belt hook, is a place to stow extra bits on the tool.

With all this extra power, make sure your drill bits and socket adapters are up to the task. Most impact drivers have a $1/4$-inch hex-shaped chuck. That's a lot of torque being applied to a thin-shanked bit or driver. Impact-rated driver bits and sockets are easy enough to find at home centers and on the Web, and they last much longer than the standard sockets or bits.

MULTIBIT SCREWDRIVER

You're up on a ladder changing the paddles on your ceiling fan, and you realize whoever installed it used whatever was around for screws. Lucky for you you've got a compact and versatile screwdriver in your back pocket. Now you don't have to make another trip up and down the ladder and rifle through your toolbox to get just the right driver—it's all in the palm of your hand. That's certainly one advantage to having a multitasking tool.

Many multibit screwdrivers are armed with magnetized, interchangeable tips, which are handy when you want to get a screw started or don't want it to drop. They are also handy at fishing a screw out of a tight spot. But you need to be careful around delicate and magnetically sensitive electronics with a magnetized tip.

Handy for a quick repair around the house, the real potential in this compact tool is when storage space is limited, like when camping, fishing, or cycling. This tool earns its keep because the screwdriver tip should match the head of whatever screw you're turning and having so many options in a tight spot is a good thing

THE RIGHT TWIST *Trying to decide which multibit screwdriver is right for you? There are several special features you should look out for. Craftsman's Autoloading model, for example, introduces the ability to switch bits without touching them; the 7-in-1 Twist-a-Nut from Ideal Industries includes a wire-nut wrench on the base of the handle; and Klenk Tool's Select-A-Bit screwdriver (pictured) features extra-long 3" bits that store in its handle. Whichever model you decide upon, make sure you're able to use it while standing on a ladder!*

SELECT-A-BIT™

PIPE WRENCH

A pipe wrench may not be versatile, but when you need to hold a pipe and fittings, nothing else will work. The body is rigid and heavy, and the teeth bite forcefully into smooth, round surfaces. When working with delicate plumbing, wrap the pipe with a leather strap or some rags to prevent the wrench from damaging it. Though most pipe wrenches are cast iron, spring for a lighter aluminum model if you face a long day of plumbing.

Daniel Stillson, a steamboat firefighter, invented this useful tool and patented it in 1869. It was referred to as a Stillson wrench until its patent expired. When using a pipe wrench, keep the pressure on the hook jaw and turn it in the direction of the heel jaw. This movement ensures the serrated jaws will bite into the workpiece and keep the wrench from slipping. While these serrated jaws are great for gripping, they are not very useful for tightening chrome-plated pipes or thin-walled copper tubing.

Pipe wrenches aren't just for pipes. Their serrated teeth can bite into a stripped nut or bolt. Once the teeth bite in and you're turning in the right direction, the pipe wrench offers a lot of leverage to remove that smoothed-over fastener. But that's not all: don't tell any plumbers this, but this tool is great for demolition work, too. Hook that jaw around a nailed down 2 x 4, and you'll show it who's boss.

25

SOCKET WRENCH SET

Reach for a socket wrench when you need to tighten nuts and bolts or loosen frozen ones. The 1/2-inch drive is the heavy hitter of the socket wrench kingdom, followed by a switch-hitter, the 3/8-inch drive, which is big enough to do light-duty automotive work yet small enough for some appliances. Reserve the 1/4-inch drive for appliance and electronics repair.

A socket fully engages a bolt's head and equally distributes the torque, minimizing the chance of stripping it. With an extension, a socket can loosen or tighten a bolt in a narrow space, allowing you to engage the ratchet with maximum leverage. The prime advantage in using a socket wrench is speed. The ratcheting in the wrench allows you to loosen or tighten a nut or bolt without having to remove and refit the wrench with each turn.

What makes a socket wrench tick? Inside the bulbous end of the socket wrench is a gear with two step-levers, or pawls. The step-levers are responsible for which direction you turn the wrench. The lever mechanism catches into a groove and allows the wrench to lock, so you can apply force in one direction and let the wrench swing unhindered in the other. This is the heart of the tool, but it can also be its Achilles Heel. There's a lot of tension placed on these pawls during use, so you'll want them to be strong. Bargain-bin socket wrenches can spill their guts after just a few uses, and when you depend on your tools to get you through your workday, it pays to buy the best you can afford. If you're at a loss as to which brand to buy, call a mechanic. Most mechanics are willing to talk shop and give you some insight. Snap-On Tools or Craftsman are a safe bet.

TONGUE AND GROOVE PLIERS

Howard Manning, chief engineer for the Champion DeArment Tool Company, invented tongue and groove pliers in 1933, improving on standard designs by adding length and leverage and increasing the jaw width. The new tool caught on among car mechanics, who used it to repair water pumps.

In 1953, the company's engineers redesigned the tongue and groove, undercutting the tongue to give the tool a firmer bite—a tweak that prevents it from slipping and busting your knuckles. They've made other improvements over the years, but the instantly recognizable grip color—probably the only hand tool color ever trademarked—has remained the same.

"Back in the early 1950s, all the pliers manufacturers started putting colored PVC (polyvinyl chloride) on their grips," says Bill DeArment, great-grandson of the company's founder. Crescent chose red; Stanley Tools, yellow. DeArment's father and uncle picked a beautiful sky blue that no one else had—and the company has used that color since 1956. In 1962, Champion changed its name to Channellock; DeArment is the president and CEO. And today, tongue and groove pliers are an essential for mechanics, farmers, plumbers, and average Joes everywhere.

TWIST AND PULL *These irreplaceable pliers are the first tool plumbers reach for when they need to grab, pull, twist, hold, tighten, or loosen something. We suggest getting two different sizes so you're ready for anything: a 10 inch and a 12 inch.*

27

MEASURING

& MARKING

AWL

A single measuring tape indicates the length of everything from lumber to copper, but when it comes time to mark those measurements, the tool to use depends on the material. Keeping the line clear and legible is one of the keys to an accurate cut. Keep an awl in your toolbox, and you'll be ready for any surface when you need to make your mark.

The most common of these tools is a scratch awl. A scratch awl is a layout tool used for marking when a pencil or marker either leaves a line that's too thick or won't leave a mark at all on the chosen workpiece. Honed to a fine point, a scratch awl is an extremely precise marking tool reserved for when craftsmen are working with tight tolerances. To use one, place a straightedge next to the awl where you need to make your mark. Angle the awl so the point is against the straightedge, then pull the scratch awl toward you along the straightedge. One thing about using an awl is that once you've made your cut line, you can't erase it. An awl's point is less likely to wander than a knife blade's if you are marking hardwoods, sheet metal, or leather, and is a staple in many shops.

There are two basic varieties: awls with a slender shaft and a delicate tip, and the more robust models, with a broad tip and a shank like a screwdriver. The first is used by woodworkers and metalworkers to scribe a sharp line; the other is used by electricians and other tradesmen to mark lines, poke holes, and scratch off rust and dirt. Depending on your needs, stock just one or both.

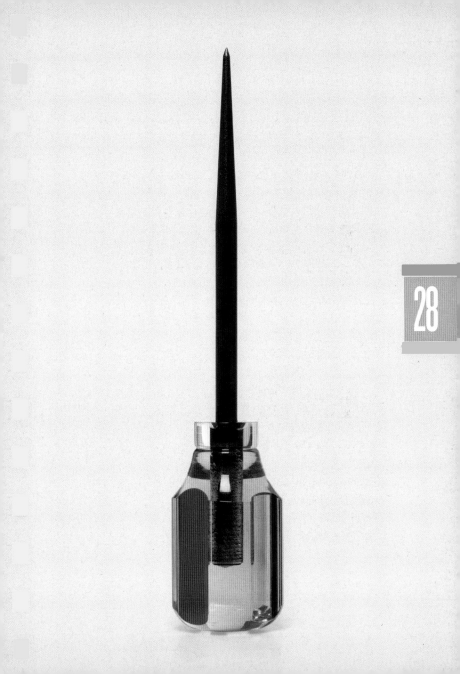

28

CARPENTER'S SQUARE

A carpenter's square, also called a steel square or framing square, has been helping builders for the better part of forever. An L-shaped wonder, this tool is terrific for laying out rafters and stairs. There are two parts to this tool. The 2-inch-wide, 24-inch-long segment is the body of the square and where you'll find the rafter tables and ruler etched in. The thinner and shorter section is called the tongue. The tongue measures 16 inches from the heel to the tip and is used to mark the plumb, or vertical, for example, cuts on rafters.

Stair buttons, sold separately, are hexagonal brass buttons which are clamped onto the square's body and tongue at exact points to ensure consistency when marking stair stringers or when laying out rafters. These brass buttons act as stops for the square, so your layout is as accurate as possible.

When buying a carpenter's square, you've got a choice between aluminum and steel. Either one works fine. Don't buy chrome; a matte or painted finish will be easier to read in bright light. Having the increments etched into the blade is the best choice since this tool gets slid, flipped, and used on a number of surfaces, and you don't want them to wear off. While this is a pretty tough square, it isn't impervious to damage. A good drop will knock it out of square, as will twisting it. Handle it like the precision instrument it is designed to be.

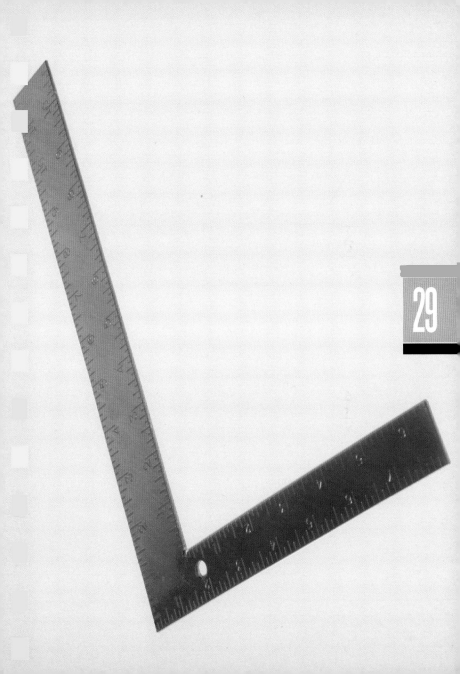

29

CENTER PUNCH

In theory, you use a center punch to start holes in metal. In practice, it's far more useful. You can tighten a loose handle on a knife or shovel by centering the punch on the rivet and then firmly striking it with a ball-peen hammer, expanding the rivet's head. In a pinch, you can also use a center punch like a steel pencil to mark a line on wood or metal, or countersink a large nail head or drive down the stub of a broken nail or staple.

While the old-school tool required some finesse, today's spring-loaded center punches take the hammer swing out of the equation (and save your bruised knuckles). Adjust the tension cap on the punch to the type of material you're working with, place the center punch onto your marked workpiece, and the punch works just like clicking a pen.

You'll want the head start for your drill bit when working with metal or dense woods. The precise indentation gives some initial bite and lowers the risk of having your drill bit walk across the surface of your workpiece, marring it. A spring-loaded center punch is ideal for starting screw holes for things like hinges, hasps, and drawer pulls.

PACK THE RIGHT PUNCH *To use this handy tool, you will set its point on dead center and strike the punch with a hammer. If the mark is not accurate, angle the punch towards the true center, tap it to extend the mark in that direction, and then mark the center again.*

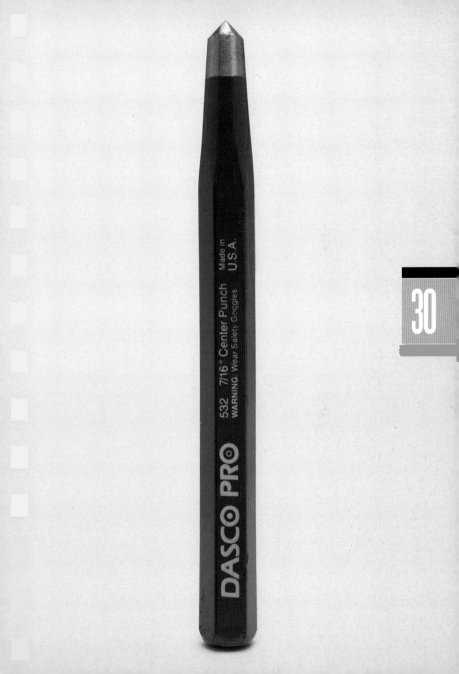

30

CHALK LINE

As technology goes, the chalk line is quite simple: a cranked spool of string that runs through a reservoir of powdered chalk. But nothing fancy works better for marking a straight line when ripping long boards, cutting drywall, or laying out the position of wall plates while framing.

If you don't have a helper to hold the other end of the chalk line for you and the hook end won't hold, just make a notch in the wood or drywall with a razor knife, then cinch the line into the cut. Then it's just a matter of pulling the string tight like a bow string and letting go.

Not all chalk is the same. The reliable standard is blue chalk, since it is easy to see and to remove. Red chalk is nearly permanent and can stand up to some weathering, but for truly permanent marking, use dark blue, crimson, or black. If you're working with fresh concrete and don't want it to get stained, skip the colors and stick to white chalk as long as the concrete is dark enough that you'll get some contrast. For interior work like aligning wallpaper or trim details, white chalk is preferable, as it's the easiest to remove and won't bleed through your work.

When the time comes to remove your mark, don't wipe it; you'll smear it into the work. Instead blow on the chalk. And don't mix colors in the reservoir. If you need to switch colors, you're better off buying another chalk line.

31

COMBINATION SQUARE

Used for marking out, measuring, and testing the squareness of corners, this versatile and useful tool was invented by Laroy Starrett in 1877. Even today, the Starrett combination square is the Rolls Royce of these tools.

This shop tool is used for marking, measuring, laying out, tuning, and setting up machinery. While the 12-inch blade (the ruler portion) is the most common size, many manufacturers produce squares with a small 4-inch blade up to a 24-inch blade.

We suggest looking for a matte finish on the ruler. While chrome looks great in a display case, it won't under strong shop lights or when the sun is shining brightly. Look for a forged-steel head or cast-iron head rather than a plastic one. The forged steel is going to be more expensive, but it will be less brittle.

One of our favorites is the Starrett Combination Set (435 Series). Not a budget tool; it's a versatile three-in-one with a 12-inch combination square which comes with a centering head and a reversible, adjustable protractor head. And its head is made out of durable cast iron to boot.

For maximum precision, first position your pencil (or the scratch awl stored in the head), then gently slide the square to the pencil (or awl) and strike your line. Check the tool's accuracy by marking a line 90 degrees to a straightedge. Flip the square and make another mark next to the first. If the two lines are not parallel, the square is off by half the discrepancy. We suggest that you buy the best instrument you can afford and set it aside for demanding precision work.

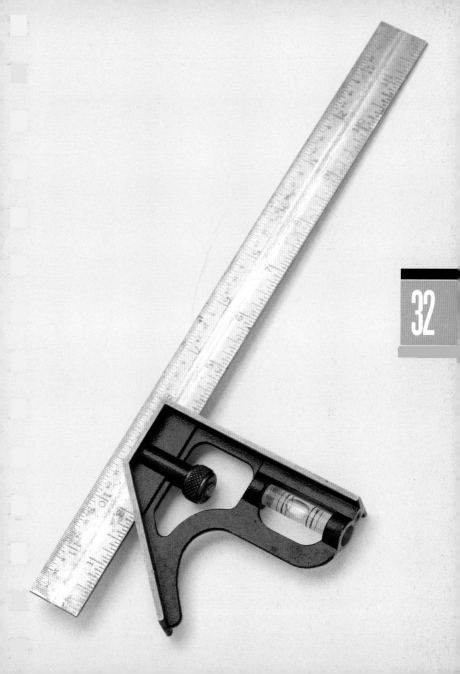

32

LEVEL

There's a level for every job, and no downside to having more than a few of this essential tool. At a minimum, your toolbox should have a 2-foot and a 9-inch torpedo level. You'll reach for the most commonly used level, the 2-foot or 4-foot, all the time. Not only will you'll use it for big projects like leveling appliances or bookshelves, it comes with a bonus: long levels make a nice straightedge.

For small jobs, pull out the pocket-sized 9-inch torpedo level, perfect for hanging pictures or setting shelves. Many torpedo levels have a magnetized side, and the vials have markings not just for level but for pitching drainpipes as well. But far be it from us to limit your level collection to just these two. Here are three more levels we suggest.

Use a line level when building a deck, fence, or any other long spanning job. It's designed to hang on a string with two small hooks and is so light it won't bow the string.

A post level can be strapped to deck piers, columns, or flag poles for hands-free plumbing. The 90-degree bend in the level reads plumb front to back and side to side simultaneously.

Finally, a self-leveling laser level can be a great choice for projects like installing a chair rail in a large room or a mud sill to a concrete foundation. Simply mount it on a stand and the laser will rotate a full 360 degrees, projecting a visible level line in any size room. Visual and audible alarms alert the user when it is beyond the leveling range.

33

SPEED SQUARE™

A lickety-split crosscutting fence for a circular saw is just one function of this terrific little tool. It's actually a rafter angle square. The name Speed Square is the registered trademark of the Swanson Tool Company. It was invented by Albert J. Swanson in 1925, and he dubbed the name Speed Square because it provides a shortcut for measurements and angle calculations. In fact, it is the preferred square for marking rafter angles, over and above the framing square.

You'll be hard pressed to find a carpenter without an apron-handy 7-inch version of this tool. For marking crosscuts and layout lines, these tools are a breeze to use, and many have notches to help guide a pencil point for marking a long rip in wood. This tool is terrific for quickly zeroing in a chop saw simply by checking the blade against the fence: lay the square against the back fence to make sure the blade is aligned for a 90-degree cut, then set the square on the miter saw's bed to check that the blade is perpendicular. Now your portable precision saw is ready for work. And another nice thing about this square: when you drop it—and it will happen—you can bet it will stay true, thanks to the strength of a triangle. Try that with a combination square or L-shaped framing square.

These squares come in two sizes. The 7-inch is a handy apron accessory, while the 12-inch version is the go-to tool for rafter and stair layouts. And don't sweat rafter calculations. Better models come with a great reference guide on how to get the most out of this must-own tool.

34

TAPE RULE

A measuring tape is a spring-loaded marvel, combining compactness, accuracy, and speed. A 25-foot model is sufficiently long to handle most home construction projects, yet small and light enough to stash in a nail pouch or clip to your jeans. But there's more to consider.

Locking devices keep the tape from rewinding. A slide lock is at the front of the tape rule; it's easy to reach and rarely unlocks unexpectedly. A lever lock performs the same function but is located on the base of the tool. A lever lock is easier to engage than a slide lock, but some people complain it's too easy to accidentally unlock the blade when in use.

Stanley's Fat Max tape is one beefy tape. The blade is an inch and a quarter wide, and combined with its concave shape, it can be horizontally extended for 11 feet without support. This extra strength is appreciated when you are measuring for crown molding or finding the right spot to hang a ceiling fan. The tape itself is easy to read. The half, quarter, and sixteenth scales are clearly marked, and there's no metric conversion on the other side of the scale to confuse the user.

The hook at the end of the tape is supposed to shift a bit. It's designed to move the distance of its own thickness. This ensures that inside measurements will be exactly the same as if you hooked it on the end of a board. To keep that hook from getting damaged, don't let that tape whip close; slow the retraction speed with your finger, and you'll keep that tape a good long time.

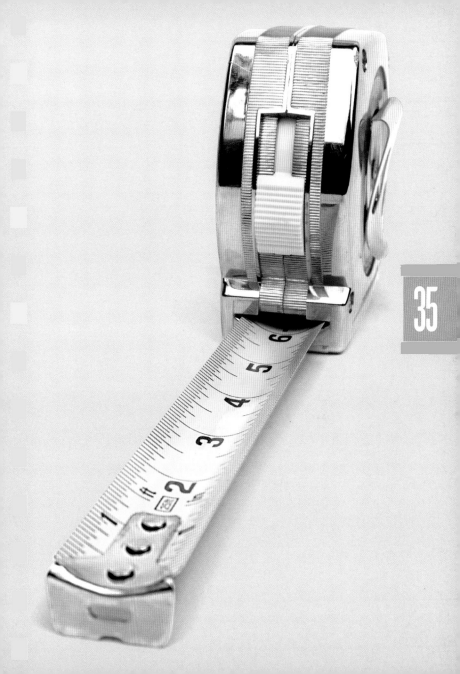

35

MULTI

PURPOSE

5-IN-1 TOOL

This jack-of-all-trades tool has a 5/64-inch-thick blade. It's a scraper, putty knife, pick, paint roller squeegee, and can opener, and some 6-in-1 models have a metal cap on the end of the handle for bumping in loose drywall nails.

The pointy pick is great for cleaning out crevices, starting an edge to remove old caulking, pulling staples, and even cleaning off a boot sole. The forward flat edge works great as a paint scraper, and you can ease it behind a delicate piece of trim you want to remove. The short flat side is perfect for prying open a can of paint, urethane, or stain. Wrap the tool in a cloth, and you can soak up a spill in the slenderest crack. The blade is stiff and wide enough for applying putty, wood filler, or joint compound to small imperfections.

Flip the tool over, and you've got a tap hammer to set the paint can's lid back in place. And that little pick on the side is great at removing dried paint that would interfere with getting that lid sealed.

The polished blade makes cleaning these tools pretty easy, but best of all is the tool's portability. It slips smoothly into your back pocket. And, of course, there's the price. You can purchase this handy tool practically anywhere and budget models start at $5. Keep your eyes peeled for the alternate version 6-in-1 (which incorporates that drywall nail setter).

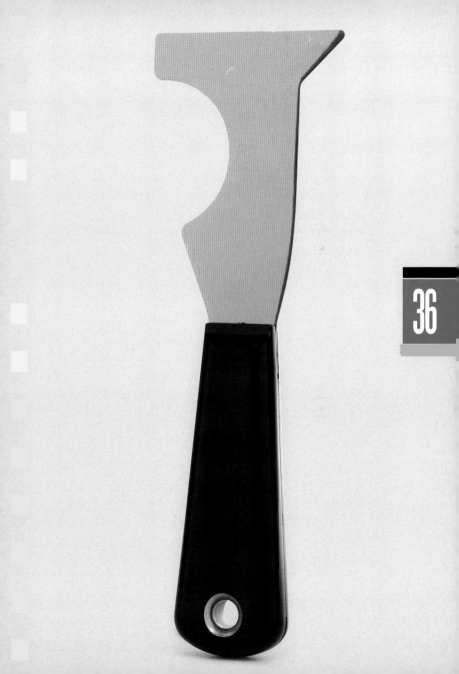

AIR COMPRESSOR

More than a tool for inflating tires, an air compressor is an invaluable alternate power source for your shop.

Years ago, it was common for shops to have a central power source that drove all the tools through a system of belts, wheels and driveshafts. The power was routed around the work space by mechanical means. While the belts and shafts may be gone, many shops still use a mechanical system to move power around the shop. It's based on the energy stored in air that's under pressure, and the heart of the system is the air compressor.

You'll find air compressors used in a wide range of situations—from corner gas stations to major manufacturing plants. And, more and more, air compressors are finding their way into home workshops, basements and garages. Models sized to handle every job, from inflating pool toys to powering tools such as nail guns, sanders, drills, impact wrenches, staplers and spray guns are now available through local home centers, tool dealers and mail-order catalogs.

The big advantage of air power is that each tool doesn't need its own bulky motor. Instead, a single motor on the compressor converts the electrical energy into kinetic energy. This makes for light, compact, easy-to-handle tools that run quietly and have fewer parts that wear out. When choosing a compressor, make sure it can supply the amount of air and the pressure that your tools need. Check the cfm (cubic feed per minute) and psi (pounds per square inch) ratings.

ANGLE GRINDER

Good for grinding metal, this often-overlooked tool has a myriad of uses. It is great at cutting, polishing, or filing metal. For hardscaping projects like cutting brick or bluestone, simply install a diamond wheel, and you can make some intricate designs and patterns out of stone. Angle grinders are also handy tile tools: they don't just cut tile; you can also use them to make repairs in an existing tile field.

And, we're just getting started with things you can do with these tools. This machine will let you put an edge on a lawnmower blade that's tackled a few too many stones. If your round nose shovel just isn't cutting the turf, it's a quick fix with this machine. Hoes, picks, and any garden implement with a blunted edge can get a quick tune-up from an angle grinder.

Rusty metal, flaking paint, crumbled mortar, or spalled concrete: the grinder has a wheel to deal with any of these obstacles. If you need to cut an old bolt, a hacksaw might take a while, but with an angle grinder, it'll just take a few seconds.

When buying an angle grinder, look for a tool that will pull 5 amps or better. With power tools, more amps equals more power. Many of these tools have a switch at the head. This can be a bit cumbersome, and we think a paddle switch that runs the length of the tool, like a long trigger, offers more control. The paddle also works as a great kill switch, if you ever drop the tool. It just shuts down, and that's a great safety measure. As with using any tool turning at nearly 10,000 rpm and shooting a rooster tail of bright orange sparks, wearing a pair of heavy-duty leather gloves and eye protection is an absolute must.

BALL-PEEN HAMMER

The face of a ball-peen hammer strikes cold chisels and punches, while the dome-shaped end rolls over the edges of rivets (peening) or works curved sheet metal. The hammer ranges in size from 4 to 50 ounces (with large models serving as blacksmiths' hammers), but the 16-ounce size works well and fits in a crowded toolbox.

A ball-peen (or ball-pein) won't chip when used against metal tools, unlike a carpenter's claw hammer, which is designed to strike relatively soft metal (namely, a nail). The tool is ideal for shaping metal, and the peen end is ideally suited for thinning metal when you want the metal to move out in all directions.

When fixing a damaged body panel on a car, the ball-peen hammer's shape lets you tap out dents to reshape and repair the damage. Match the head size as closely as you can to the dent. Using a solid scrap of metal as a dolly on the top of the dent, you can tap the dent from behind and shape the repair. It does take some experience and finesse to work on your car, and gentle taps go a long way.

ABOUT FACE *Don't expect to be shaping metal often? Look for a hard face hammer in a light weight (8 to 12 ounces). You'll use this versatile tool often when chiseling or working with metal sheets. But if you'll be working with soft metals like bronze or copper, you need a soft face ball-peen, made of brass, plastic, or lead. Unfortunately, soft face hammers will wear out over time, so be prepared to replace the head.*

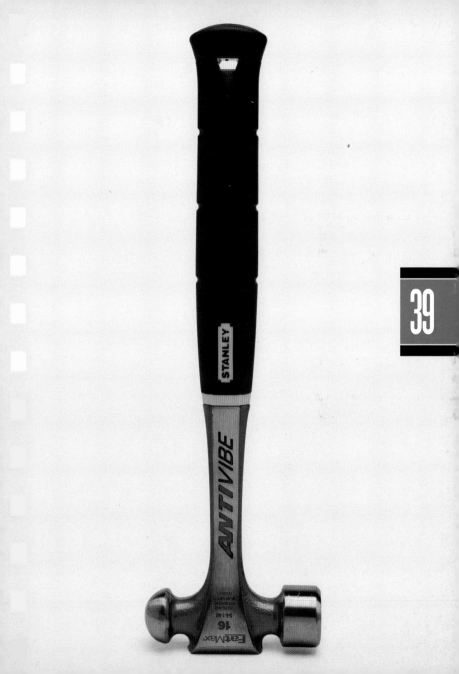

39

BOW RAKE

Rugged and simple, the bow rake remains the best device for raking heavy material, such as gravel or tangled sticks. The bow acts as a shock absorber, protecting your arms while you work. If you can turn it over, the straight back can also be used to level soil.

A bow rake's head can range in size from 8 to 24 inches in width. The head is connected to the handle with a steel bow that gives the tool some strength for serious raking. The head will have anywhere from 12 to 24 tines that are designed for leveling materials, spreading mulch or compost, blending fertilizer into tilled soil, or removing heavier debris.

To keep the tool tuned, make sure it is hosed off after being used. One precaution to take is to apply a spritz of WD-40 from time to time to keep rust at bay. And to protect a wooden handle, some Thompson's Water Seal around the rake head is a great precaution to stave off wood rot. Fiberglass is really the way to go with these rakes, since it is light and nearly impervious to water damage.

GET A GRIP ON THIS *Everyone should have a bow rake on hand, but it's far from the only rake you'll need. Stock a 24-inch leaf rake to help manage your yard come Autumn. And there's the compact 8-inch shrub rake if you have shrubberies, fences, or other tight spaces. Finally, a thatch rake, similar in build to the bow rake, is irreplaceable when removing thatch.*

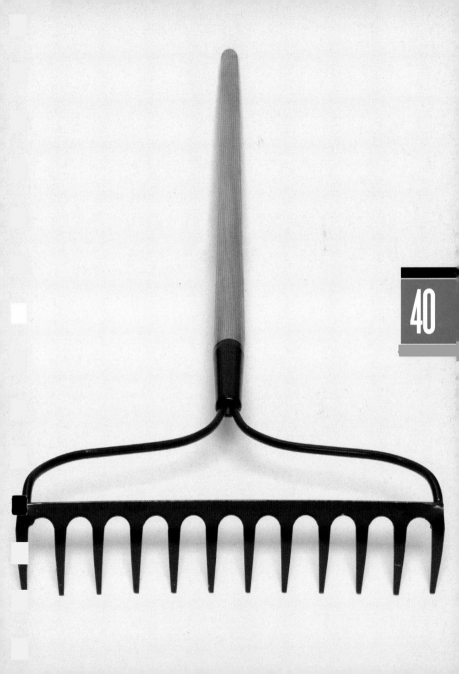

40

CLAMP

You might be able to get by with owning just one hammer, but the single-tool philosophy doesn't work when it comes to clamps. That's because there's no one clamp that's versatile enough to satisfy all of our DIY clamping chores. Fortunately, clamps come in many different styles, sizes and models—and as any woodworker will tell you, you can't have too many. From clothespins to pipe clamps that can span 10 feet or more, these tools hold things together. Here are a few of our favorites.

C-clamps get their name from their shape and are often referred to as G-clamps. By clamping a belt sander to a bench, they can transform a sander into a grinder and are ideal for honing a workpiece.

Generally used for woodworking glue-ups, bar clamps have almost limitless uses. The best innovation of late is the K-body clamp. Its jaws are encassed in a nonmarring, glue resistant material and are designed to remain parallel under pressure. The bars on these clamps are serrated on six sides to minimize slippage.

One-handed bar clamps are terrific for the lone worker and close by using a hand grip instead of by ratcheting a screw.

Spring clamps are terrific for holding tarps and just about anything else you can get the jaws around. Quick, simple, and easy to use, they should be plentiful in every shop.

Keep in mind that you may need to buy several of the same type of clamp—various sizes of C-clamps or spring clamps, for example—but one miter clamp or band clamp is usually sufficient.

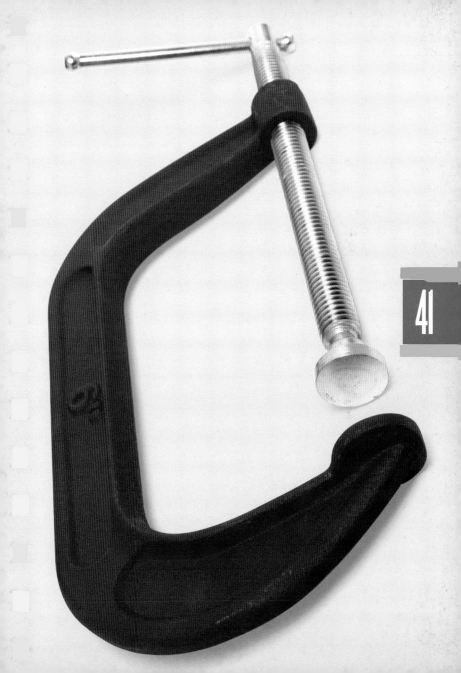

41

CORDLESS DRILL

Cordless drills readily combine speed, power, and portability— so for most of us, they've already replaced the corded variety. They also come with a clutch that disconnects the drive mechanism when it reaches a dialed-in force setting, preventing the user from stripping the screw.

The lithium-ion batteries of today's models allow these tools to be both light and workhorses, too. While the 14- to 18-volt models can handle most jobs, some drills have voltages in the mid-20s or even 30s for power that rivals that of the corded product.

If you'll be working on plumbing and running wire, a right-angle drill will make your life easier. You won't have to squeeze the drill and the bit between studs or joist bays any longer. A right-angle drill has a compact head and slim body for easy working in tight areas. Cabinetmakers might find this their drill of choice, since it's ideal for getting into tight spaces.

The keyless chuck is nice for quick bit changing, and the adjustable clutch means we can control the drill's torque. Many models are equipped with small lights. You might think they're a hokey accessory—until you need them.

Many cordless drills have a hammer drill function, which is necessary when you've got to get through some concrete or dense plaster. You'd be hard pressed to find people who don't drive screws or other fasteners with this tool. But when driving screws, change over from a Phillips head screw to either a square drive (Robertson) or a Torx screw. You'll be happy you did.

42

GOOSENECK BAR

This is also called a wrecking bar—for good reason. A curved neck gives this steel tool incredible prying power, perfect for separating two pieces of lumber that are nailed together. Rely on small models up to 18-inches long for light-duty demolition, and keep a 36-inch bar on hand for the really big stuff.

The gooseneck bar is a dual-headed tool. The chisel end is great for lifting heavy stones when landscaping and for prying things apart like frozen firewood. The gooseneck end usually has a split claw that's great for driving under the head of a nail that you need to remove. The curved neck provides a tremendous amount of leverage in a small amount of space.

You've probably seen these bars featured on any number of home improvement television shows. What they show is the more entertaining aspect of this tool when it's used as a striking instrument. For breaking up tile, cabinets, studs, or just about anything in the way, the impact from this lever is focused on a small striking point, usually the gooseneck bend, creating a tremendous amount of force. Wearing safety goggles is a must when using this tool, as is a warning cry like "Fore" to warn others in the area that there may be flying debris.

WRECK IT RIGHT *Use the pry bar end (near the curve) to pull out nails sticking ¼" or more out of a piece of wood. If that doesn't do it, some wrecking bars have a teardrop notch in the flat end, useful to get additional pull where necessary— a tremendous help.*

HAMMER

In 30,000 BC, someone altered the destiny of the human race by lashing a stick to a rock, a refinement that increased the user's strike speed and accuracy. The hammer was born. Later, stone begat bronze, begat iron, begat steel—a material that could be forged into a ruthlessly efficient shape. Yet, after all these millennia, the wood handle remains, preferred by craftsmen for its light weight, shock absorbency, and balance. It was the post–World War II housing boom that finally transformed the profile of the modern hammer. Can't-frame-'em-fast-enough carpenters on the West Coast needed still more speed, so they grafted elements of heavy rigging hatchets onto claw hammers. The result is the beefy, all-business, California-style framer, a swift, long-handled striking tool with a vicious claw.

Hammering is a repetitive act and lots of guys have suffered from carpenter's elbow (tennis elbow is for sissies). What's a man to do? Get a titanium hammer from Stiletto Tools. A titanium hammer is lighter than your steel-headed counterpart and offers a significant reduction in recoil and vibration while delivering more swing force where it's really needed: hitting the nail on the head. The design improvements on the tool include a magnetic nail starting slot, a side nail puller, and a rubberized titanium handle. They still make wooden-handled hammers with titanium heads, but these newer handles are slightly curved and specifically engineered to improve your striking force with a lot less effort. Titanium hammers are expensive, but once you heft one, it'll be tough to put it back.

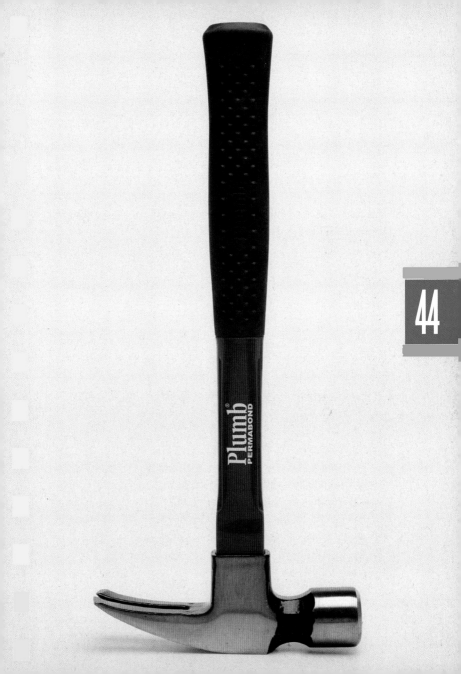

44

HAND TRUCK

Once you own a hand truck, you'll wonder how you got along without it. Unfortunately, like owning a pickup truck, having a hand truck becomes an open invitation to help someone who's moving. If you find yourself carrying heavy things with some frequency and need to be mobile at the same time, then you'll find this tool irreplaceable.

Some hand trucks are small, lightweight, collapsible models, terrific for small loads like briefcases and camera equipment, and are occasionally found at airports used by frequent travelers hauling heavy luggage.

But what about the serial remodeler? Tool totes and boxes get heavy pretty quickly, as do table saws and chop saws. While many manufacturers make tools that have wheels, many of us own tools that don't, and these are awkward to carry. Some are just downright heavy. Strapping them down to a hand truck makes them easy to set up and break down—and at the end of a fast-paced day in the sun, wouldn't it be nice to roll the tools back to the shop rather than carry them?

Damaged knees and compromised backs are no strangers to hands-on types, and a hand truck is a common-sense addition to anyone who has injured them or those wanting to avoid such problems in the future. Pick up the model that would work best for you—we suggest taking an inventory of your workshop to weigh the heaviest item you'll require a hand truck for.

45

MACHINIST VISE

Whether stationary or swiveling, a vise is like an extra set of (really strong) hands for securing your work. Cast-iron models function well for most applications, but buy a forged-steel vise for anything heavy-duty. If you cut a lot of pipe, choose a vise with V-shaped jaws to grip round material, but be careful not to overtighten the pipe. You'll knock it out of round. For moderate metal pounding, choose one with an anvil behind the jaws. While it's no substitute for a blacksmith anvil, it is handy for small projects.

When using a vise for wood projects, pad the jaws with wood scraps and don't overtighten the jaws. Otherwise, you run the risk of compressing the wood fibers, which can lead to cracking or splitting your workpiece.

A swiveling vise is a more versatile tool, since you move the tool to suit your needs and not the other way around. But a machinist vise doesn't have to stay in the shop attached to a bench. Most plumbers and welders will have one attached to the bumper of their work truck, turning the truck bed into a veritable mobile workshop. They keep the vise from rusting with a liberal amount of WD-40, a wire brush, and a large plastic freezer bag as a cover.

GRIP OF STEEL *Our favorite heavy-duty vise has a 4-inch jaw spread and an anvil for whacking stuff into place: Irwin's 226304. Use it for everything from home welding and steel cutting to clamping bar stock. A swivel base is for optimum positioning; the built-in pipe clamp is tuned for working round stock.*

46

METAL FILE

Bake it in a cake, and you've got a tool to cut jail bars, but put it into the hands of a craftsman, and it's a veritable magic wand. With metal files, there are two basic cutting designs: the single-cut file and the double-cut file.

The teeth on a single-cut file are in rows and are the best choice for smoothing. Double-cut files have teeth in a diamond pattern and remove more material per pass, leaving a rougher surface in their wake. Both types of files come in a variety of tooth size (smaller teeth, which correlates to more tpi (teeth per inch), will produce a smoother cut for a finer finish). The most common-sized metal file is the bastard file, which has 26 tpi. This is a good all-around file since it's neither too rough nor too smooth. Smoothing files range in tooth count from 60 tpi to what's known as a dead smooth file, which has 100 tpi. Rougher-cut files like the second-cut file have 36 tpi, and coarse files have 16 tpi.

Files also come in a number of different shapes, but for most uses, a flat, double-cut bastard file is considered the go-to tool. A rat-tail, or round file, is the right choice for sharpening serrated-edge tools.

When using a metal file, grasp the handle with one hand and grasp the point, or head, of the file with the other hand. Place the middle face of the file on your workpiece, and with a little pressure at the point of the file, push it across the surface you're smoothing. Use as much of the file per stroke as you can, then lift the file and start again without making contact on the return stroke.

47

NEEDLE-NOSE PLIERS

When you need to fish a dropped screw out of a tight space or when working on electronics, there's nothing handier than a pair of needle-nose pliers. Their elegant shape is also perfect for fastening a wire to a switch or an outlet receptacle: grip the wire at the tip of the jaws and roll the pliers to produce a neat hook, then fasten the hook under the terminal screw. These pliers also serve in a pinch as a cutting tool for small gauge wire.

Like any tool, you can find a myriad of uses for needle-nose pliers. Because the nose of the pliers is long and thin and has a knurled or crosshatched tip, it's easy to hold a brad or finishing nail and hammer it without hurting your fingers. For hanging picture hooks or doing any such small operations, it's a great advantage to drive the nail while keeping your hands out of the way. If you're nailing small trim details, it helps to either predrill for the fastener at your workbench or dull its tip by whacking it once with a hammer.

ON THE NOSE *So, just how many of these little wonders should you have around? We recommend one for each hand, and at least one very small pair—more if your wife does any crafts with beads or jewelry. In addition to the straight-nose version, pick up a pair of bent-nose pliers. You never know when you'll need them.*

48

PRY BAR

Shorter and flatter than a gooseneck bar, a pry bar is most useful for removing trim and paneling. Many variations exist, but the most versatile types have at least one nail-pulling slot (two is better).

These pry bars, also known as flat bars, are arched along the body to provide gentle leverage along the long side of the tool, which is handy when relieving the weight of a door to slip hinge pins or when installing the bottom sheet of drywall and cinching the sheet up that extra inch or two to get a tight seam. If you need an extra inch of lift, slip a block of wood under the tool and you've got a tough, yet handy, lift. Roofers use pry bars to strip shingles, and renovators use them for all sorts of lighter demolition work.

Typically each chiseled end has a nail-pulling slot, and the steep curved end is pretty tough and can take being hit with a hammer. Many models also offer a teardrop slot, which accommodates the smallest nails. This slot serves two functions: One is for pulling even the slimmest finishing nail. The other is to steady a brad or other small fastener, which keeps fumbling fingers out of the hammer's way and also shields the wood from a misaligned hammer blow.

Most pry bars are made of steel, and they hold up very well. Titanium pry bars are making their way to the market, too. These bars are lighter, just as strong, and deliver less vibration to the user. Look for one with a staple-pulling tab, which is handy for shingle removal and on flooring.

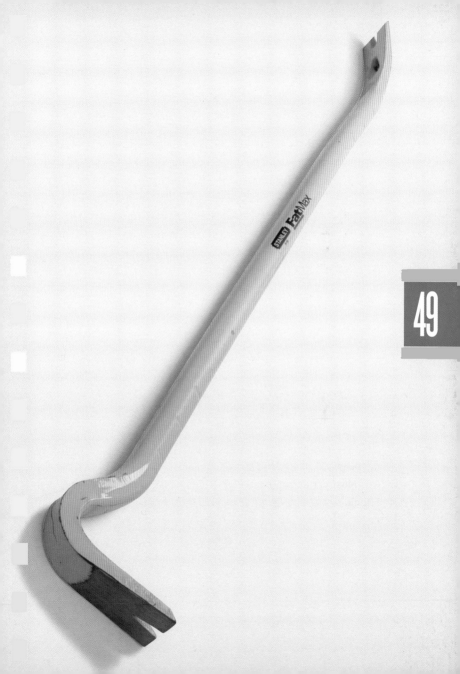

49

PUTTY KNIFE

The putty knife is more than a single implement. Rather, it's a group of tools, ranging from knives with flexible, thin blades to heavy-duty models that are ground with a tip like a chisel (which, not surprisingly, are called chisel-edge putty knives).

You can get by with one or two. A thinner 1-inch-wide stiff blade works wonders on jobs like glazing windows and filling nail holes, while a more flexible 4-inch-wide knife comes in real handy for small drywall repairs, like a ding from a child's thrown toy.

A 1-inch blade typically has a chisel-shaped bevel point (pictured) and a thick ($5/64$-inch) high-carbon steel blade. The flexible 4-inch skiff has a thinner blade ($1/32$-inch), but is still made of high-carbon steel.

Never apply wood filler with your finger, because it will mold to the wood's surface, announcing the nail hole instead of concealing it. Instead, use the 1-inch knife to apply the putty and then remove the excess putty by drawing the blade in the opposite direction of application. If you're working on a wood surface that is going to be stained, reach for a flexible-bladed putty knife, especially when working with softer woods like pine or cedar. With a flexible blade, you're less likely to damage a fragile surface.

Better tools have a high-carbon steel blade. Reserve using those plastic disposable ones for working with a two-part auto body filler, the no-scuff application of putty on painted surfaces, or an epoxy reserved for exterior repairs, such as porch columns or window sills that have suffered some rot.

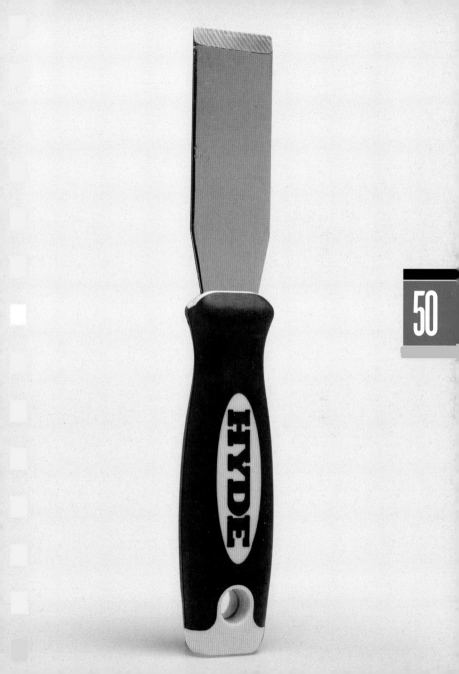

50

RANDOM ORBITAL SANDER

If you are in the market to buy just one sander, pick up a random orbital sander. This tool combines orbital motion with rotation and, armed with the right sandpaper, can handle almost any job requiring abrasive action, from stripping paint to producing a nearly mirror finish on wood or metal. If you've got a lot of material to remove, use a belt sander.

Random orbital sanders come in three sizes. Palm sanders are for light-duty finish work. A pistol grip sander is for heavier work. Large right-angle sanders are for smoothing large surfaces, like floors and table tops. Many models offer variable speeds as well as orbit modes for fine finishing or more aggressive action.

Look for a tool that has a vacuum adapter, so you can connect it to your shop vac. This is a great addition to the tool, since you're significantly reducing airborne hazards by directing the dust into the shop vac instead of letting it settle all over the place. While just about every random orbital sander does have a dust bag, they are no match for a vacuum attachment.

SMOOTH OPERATOR *In addition to the vacuum adapter, you'll need to select which of two sanding disks best suits your needs. We recommend going with the hook-and-loop system over the pressure-sensitive adhesive disc. The hook-and-loop, while a bit more expensive, allows the user to quickly and easily switch grits and reuse discs that aren't yet worn out.*

51

ROPE

Rope is used to hold objects in place, to lift things, to tow them, for a kid's swing, and for safety lines when people work up high. So it's important to choose a rope that has the strength and durability for your specific job.

For general use, not safety or climbing, a few things to consider are a rope's minimum breaking strength (a theoretical value) and its minimum working load limit, a more realistic number that helps you determine if the rope is suited for the job. One or both may be included on the rope's package. To be more precise, see the handy guide produced by the Cordage Institute that helps you determine how to safely use rope.

Natural fiber rope is great for general use, but for outdoor use, look for one that's specially treated for water. Natural fibers tend to swell when wet and stiffen once they dry. They are also susceptible to rotting. Polyester ropes are ideal for most outdoor applications.

Cutting rope isn't hard, but there's a trick to keep the ends from unraveling. Simply wrap the area you want to cut with a durable tape—duct tape comes to mind—and cut with a sharp knife. The tape will keep the ends from coming undone.

For climbing, caving, or as safety lines, kernmantle rope is unsurpassed. Besides knotting easily, it's dynamic. If you happen to fall, a kernmantle rope will stretch to gradually absorb the impact. The rate of stretch is about 10 percent, or 5 feet of stretch for every 50 feet of rope. The reason for this built-in braking system is that it lessens the jolt a climber or roofer will suffer from a sudden stop if they happen to fall.

52

ROUND NOSE SHOVEL

The round nose shovel digs, cuts, and pries, but like any tool, its efficiency depends on you. Start with the shovel perpendicular to the soil, and use your weight and leg muscles, not your arms, to drive it down. To toss dirt, hold the shovel close and keep your forward hand on the blade socket. Bend both knees. If you're right-handed, point your left foot in the direction of the toss.

Because you'll be placing your foot on what's called the shovel's shoulder (the flat part of the head perpendicular to the handle), we suggest looking for a shovel with a wider shoulder, to distribute the digging force. Try to use your heel and not the arch of your foot.

Buy a good-quality shovel and it will last you a long time. Look for one with a stainless-steel blade, but in a pinch, alloy steel will last reasonably well. No matter the length of the handle (more on that later) you'll need to select a strong hardwood, such as ash or hickory, or a reinforced fiberglass shaft. The handle should be riveted with metal plates on its crosspiece. Make sure the hollow shaft socket and blade are forged in one piece.

HANDLE IT RIGHT *There's more than just one version of this irreplaceable tool. We suggest stocking two versions of it: a long handle and the shorter, D-handle. A longer handle will give you more leverage for tasks like prying out a stubborn root or a good-sized stone, and the short D-handled shovel is terrific where space is at a premium.*

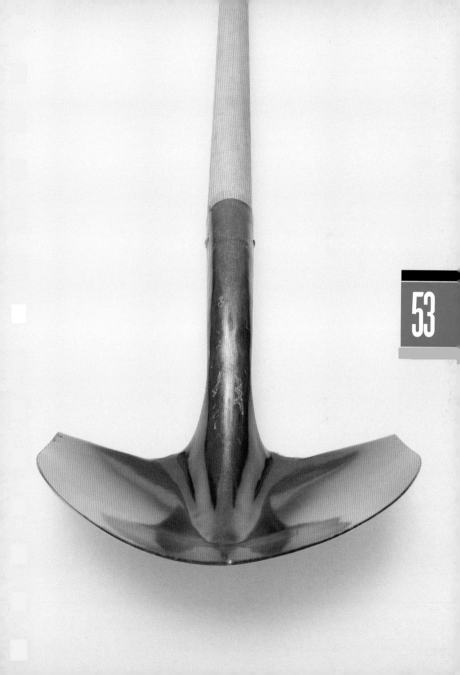

53

SAW HORSES

One mark of a craftsman is the ability to make a sturdy pair of stackable saw horses. The choice of lightweight but sturdy materials is as much a component as the execution of the compound angles or the selection of additional features, such as braces, slots, and shelves. It was a carpenter's calling card once upon a time, and for some it still is.

A pair of saw horses can be used as a temporary work table, holding lumber for cutting, and as tool stands. And making them yourself is its own reward. You should plan to spend a few hours making them, but it will be worth it.

Using 8 x $5/4$ stock for the top, simply scribe and notch the lumber for the legs to fit. Legs are reinforced with a gusset plate that also acts as a support for the top, making them real workhorses. Whenever you make a wood-to-wood connection, remember this mantra: Screws and glue always prove true.

PLY ME A RIVER *Available at our Web site (found at www.popularmechanics.com) under Home How-To are detailed blueprints and step-by-step instructions on how to build several types of saw horses. Our classic design is sturdy and versatile, providing a wide work surface and legs angled in two directions for stability. Two alternate designs (both faster to build) are also provided: a rugged two-by-four saw horse with legs splayed at 20 degrees; and a hinged, lightweight model suitable for supporting trim and wood pieces for painting and staining.*

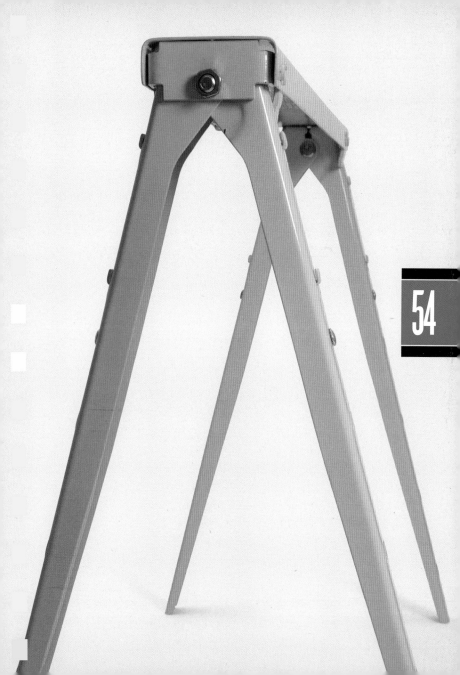

54

SHOP VACUUM

They look like small garbage cans on wheels, and their appetite for workshop waste is nothing short of voracious. Designed to pick up debris a household vac would choke on in seconds, wet-dry vacs also inhale liquids with blinding speed and have cleanup compartments measured in gallons, and the mess goes into a watertight, washable drum instead of a bag.

Smaller machines typically have a 2 to 4 gallon capacity with motors around 3 horsepower. For most around-the-house cleanups, these machines are ideal. For home workshops or job sites, you'll want a larger machine. Midrange shop vacs will have 10- to 20-gallon capacities and 5-horsepower motors. These machines are pretty loud but can suck up just about anything that's not nailed down.

With a little ingenuity and PVC pipe, you can use a shop vac as a dust collection system in your home shop. Also, several manufacturers make models that work in conjunction with your power tools. Flip the switch to your router, sander, or saw, and the vacuum kicks in—which is great when you're working inside the house. The vacuum will shut off a few seconds after the tool, just to make sure that it's grabbed the last of the sawdust.

If your vacuum isn't picking up the way it used to, there's a good chance the filter is just clogged. While you can knock the dirt and dust off it up to a point, there are times when the filter just gets too worn, damp, or dirty to be effective. Replace it. You'll literally breathe easier.

55

SLEDGEHAMMER

Few tools combine brute force and finesse as elegantly as a sledgehammer. There's something therapeutic about hefting a sledge to pulverize an ugly, old brick stoop or to drive some fence posts. With a wedge and a sledge, you can split some firewood and get your own stove burning, too. Most of us are better off with an easy-to-swing 8- or 10-pound sledge with an unbreakable fiberglass handle, as opposed to a 16- to 20-pounder.

But this dynamic tool isn't just used for destructive purposes. It can be used to align the legs of a door opening. Use a sacrificial block and place it against the side you need to shift. The block will protect the framing from the destructive force of the steel head and distribute it along the wall. With a controlled knock or two, you can straighten out cross-legged door openings, salvage architectural elements, or position plywood subflooring so the sheets get snugged together without damage.

Using a sledge for any length of time can be a real workout. But, if you've got some Tom Sawyer in you, you might just convince one of the younger guys how great it feels and let them take a swing at it.

POUND IT OUT *Swinging a sledge is 10% strength and 90% skill. Position yourself with your left foot ahead of your right (for right-handers) and just right and behind your target. You'll want to arc the swing as high and tall as possible; this will let gravity provide the force behind your strike. Your right hand should begin the swing at the top of the handle, under the head, and slide down the grip to meet your left hand near its base by the impact.*

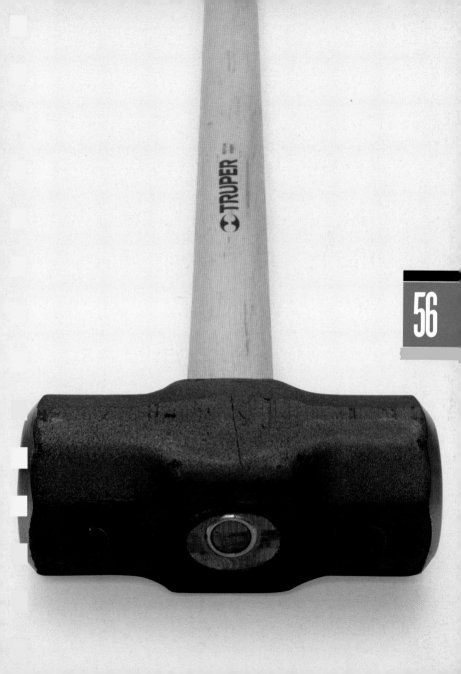

56

SQUARE NOSE SHOVEL

With a squared, flat, even edge, this is not a digging tool. It's for leveling areas for patios or walkways, for squaring ditches, and for clearing gravel, sand, or snow from surfaces. Its square-headed design makes it ideal for scooping debris and measuring material. When using it to place concrete, work the back of the blade against the inside surface of a slab form to consolidate concrete there.

Here's a great back-saving technique when creating a flat-bottomed hole with your shovel. Simply place the back face of a square-nosed shovel flat against the earth, so that the butt of the handle hits around your hips. Keep your spine straight as you walk the shovel forward, plowing forward with your leg muscles while the shovel collects the loose dirt like a dustpan.

But leveling ground isn't all this tool is good for: It can also strip roofing shingles. The flat head lets you get under roofing nails, and the leverage of the handle makes popping them out a real breeze. When removing shingles, it's best to start from the ridge and proceed down. It's also handy for remodelers, since it acts as a virtual plaster plow when run horizontally against a wall along the lathe. The long, flat blade is also handy for popping drywall off walls during demolition.

GET A HANDLE ON IT *Replacing a shovel handle is one of those disappearing rural skills that demonstrates basic mechanical competence. The most overlooked part of the job is getting the grain direction right. First, cut or grind off the rivets and slide the old handle out of the blade socket. When you mount the new handle, orient its grain so that the oval rings are to the side of the handle, not on the top or bottom (relative to the blade).*

57

STEPLADDER

The safest way to reach things inside the house is with a properly sized stepladder. Although they range in height from 3 to 20 feet, the most useful ladders are those in the 6- to 10-foot range. It should be tall enough for you to change a lightbulb but not so large as to be unwieldy. For use on stairs and uneven surfaces like driveways, ramps, or curbs, a versatile ladder like an adjustable Little Giant ladder might fit your needs.

When using a typical stepladder, you should stand at least 2 feet from the top, and the maximum working height is about 3 feet above the top of the ladder. So, a 5-foot stepladder will provide a safe and effective working height of 8 feet. Many ladder-related accidents are a result of falls, and these rules are provided to offer optimal balance for the user. The other danger with stepladders is when tools are left on the top of the ladder and then forgotten. When the ladder is later moved, the tools come raining down, and if it's a hammer or screwdriver, that can leave a mark.

These are some other rules: Do not lean to reach when you're on a stepladder. The rule of thumb is to keep your belt buckle between the ladder rails. Also, don't use a stepladder as a leaning ladder. Stepladders should only be used in a fully opened position with the side and cross braces locked. And finally, unless stated otherwise by the manufacturer, stepladders should never be used as a poor man's scaffold. Never use a stepladder to support a work platform.

VISE-GRIP

Vise-grips, also called locking pliers, are considered by many to be the very first hybrid tool. Patented in 1924 by inventor and blacksmith William Petersen, they're part pliers and part vise. Petersen realized his job as a blacksmith would be easier if he had a set of pliers that would clamp down and hold his workpiece in a vise-like grip. After experimenting with several prototypes, he developed the screw mechanism in the handle to adjust the opening of the pliers and a few years later, developed the locking handle.

The tool was popular among farmers and mechanics in Petersen's area of Nebraska. Although the Great Depression slowed his new company's growth, his small manufacturing plant was staffed by nearly forty employees. By 1941, the little plant was operating at full capacity.

Defense industries building ships and aircraft used thousands of these handy tools. Some shipbuilders, who were so strapped for time, actually welded the vise-grips into the hull of their ships. After the war, Petersen took advantage of the first National Hardware Show in 1945, where the tool was billed as the "World's Most Versatile Hand Tool."

The original tool came with a wire-cutting option, which is still available. Now, the tool comes in a variety of shapes and sizes. The familiar round nose pliers with four points of contact on bolts are still the most common and widely recognized version. There are also needle-nose and straight-jawed models as well as specialized sheet metal–working pliers. One of the more significant and recent improvements has to be the soft grip, which is a real bonus when you're working out in the cold.

59

WHEELBARROW

No other gardening device has been the subject of such intense observation and improvement, over such a long period of time, as the humble wheelbarrow or its cousin, the garden cart. Both trace their origins to the dawn of wheeled transport, and no less a mechanical authority than Thomas Jefferson made notes, comments and sketches regarding their design.

Modern wheelbarrows and carts come in almost every shape, size and material—not to mention price. The differences between carts and wheelbarrows is slight, so much so that many products today blur the line between the two. For one thing, a wheelbarrow has one or two wheels, but a cart is always a two-wheeled affair. Generally, a wheelbarrow has its wheels in front of its tray. The front wheel position (especially when it is a single wheel) gives a wheelbarrow somewhat more maneuverability than a cart and allows you to dump its contents easily. A cart, on the other hand, usually has more capacity and is more stable while being moved or loaded.

There are times when you need the toughest product you can lay your hands on. This is it. Called the C6, it's a contractor-grade wheelbarrow that consists of a 6-cubic-foot tray supported at the front with a pair of heavy uprights. A raised rim around each tray bolt prevents the edge of a shovel or mortar hoe from catching on them. The tray has a heavy, well-rounded rim and a tough, electrostatically applied paint job. The undercarriage is an assembly that locks together with hook-shaped joints and large bolts. The ash handles are lacquered for weather resistance, and the wheel bearing is oil-impregnated for maximum durability.

60

PURPOSE

CAULK GUN

A cheap caulk gun doesn't apply even pressure during the extrusion of the caulk and may affect the bead you're laying. Worse still, the caulk can literally backfire around the stopper, leaving you with a mess of wasted material on your hands. A good-quality gun, on the other hand, will cost from $8 to $12 and will prove its worth the first time you use it. There's nothing as expensive as cheap tools.

These guns keep steady pressure with a no-drip feature that actually works. The poker rod is actually long enough to puncture the nozzle seal on the tube of caulk, instead of making you cut the tube lower down on the nozzle than you want.

Caulk may be the most misused building product in the world. It is used to seal joints between adjacent building elements, like a tub and a wall. Unfortunately, caulk is often substituted for good workmanship or proper construction. It is not meant to fill large gaps; it's to ease the transition between two well-fitted building elements.

To remove old caulk, simply soften the existing caulk with a caulk remover. Then slice through the softened caulk with a sharp utility knife. The caulk should come free, but if not, a pair of needle-nose pliers will help. Rake the remaining caulk from the joint using a 5-in-1 tool. Before applying a new bead of caulk, clean the surface. If there's any mildew, a solution of $1/3$ cup of bleach to a gallon of water does the trick. Once the area is clean, apply your bead of caulk.

SPOUT CUTTER

61

DUST MASK

A dust mask provides protection against nontoxic dust and pollen and is an irreplaceable tool for anyone with a workshop. A step up are respirators, which provide protection against fumes, gases, vapors, and other harmful particles in the air. But how can you tell the difference?

An inexpensive dust mask lacks a rating by the National Institute for Occupational Safety and Health (NIOSH) and will not seal tightly against your face, allowing airborne hazards to enter your airway. For most jobs, use a disposable respirator. Respirators will have a NIOSH rating; many are given an N95 rating, which means that they are rated to filter out fine particles like soot, smoke, and ash and have a 95 percent efficiency rating against solid and liquid particles that don't contain oil. An N100 rating is even better. Sometimes Web-based retailers and others call both products by the same name, so shop carefully.

If you're sanding drywall compound, refinishing a floor, cutting cedar or black walnut, or performing any other job that creates airborne dust, then you need to protect your lungs. Although you're using a respirator, you might not have fitted it against your face properly. If you have a beard, or a couple of days' growth, the mask will not form a tight seal and particles can enter your airway. To make sure the mask is fitted properly, cover your respirator with both hands but don't press it against your face. Exhale sharply. If you feel air blowing on your face or eyes, the respirator needs to be adjusted.

62

EARMUFFS

Hearing damage is permanent, but it's also preventable. Earmuffs, as opposed to earplugs or headphones, provide maximum protection. Really loud shop tools, such as chain saws and circular saws, operate above 100 decibels—and noise higher than 85 decibels begins to cause damage. OSHA (the Occupational Safety and Health Administration) requires employers to provide hearing protection if the environment noise level exceeds 85 decibels, for example. Choose a product that has a high noise-reduction rating (NRR)—preferably in the range of 23 to 33.

While earmuffs do provide optimum protection, they have to form a soundproof seal around your ears. So wearing safety glasses or having long hair will impinge on their noise-reduction ratings. Most NRRs refer to optimal conditions, so your actual noise reduction will be somewhat less than what the product is capable of achieving in a laboratory test setting.

Earplugs are not as good at sound reduction, but they aren't compromised by safety glasses or long hair. If optimal eye and ear protection are a must, look to the setup used by many arborists for all-around safety: a headband equipped with earmuffs that also supports a full face shield and a hard hat.

HEAR THAT? *According to NIOSH and the CDC (Centers for Disease Control and Prevention), a continuous noise at 100 decibels can begin to cause damage in 15 minutes. And that exposure time is halved for every three decibels it increases—which means at 115 decibels, damage can occur in less than a minute.*

63

FETY WORKS

EXTENSION CORD

Most people buy an extension cord based on length, but there are other things to consider.

Extension cords are rated for indoor or outdoor use. The jacket, or insulation, on the outdoor-rated version is made to withstand temperature fluctuations, moisture, and UV radiation. Indoor cords aren't so hardy. Left exposed, an indoor-rated cord's insulating jacket will deteriorate, raising the risk of life-threatening shocks or fire.

Extension cords carry an amperage rating based on the wire's gauge and length. A wire's gauge measures the wire's diameter and determines how much current it can carry. The lower the gauge number, the larger the cable's diameter and the more current it can carry.

The amperage rating tells you how much current you can draw with a specific cord. If you plan on using a number of tools at one time, it's important to know how many amps you're going to be pulling. Amperage information is provided by Underwriters Laboratory and is printed on your tool. A 10-gauge 100-foot power cord is a heavy hitter and should be your choice if you are using high-amperage tools farther than 50 feet from your power source. For a 50-footer, look for a 12-gauge 15-amp cord. For most jobs at 25 feet from the power outlet, a 14-gauge cord with a 15-amp rating should do the job.

148

ADD MORE JUICE *While the extension cord's amp rating should match up to your tools, we suggest going up one wire gauge size when in doubt. It's best to use a cord with a little extra amp capacity (also known as ampacity).*

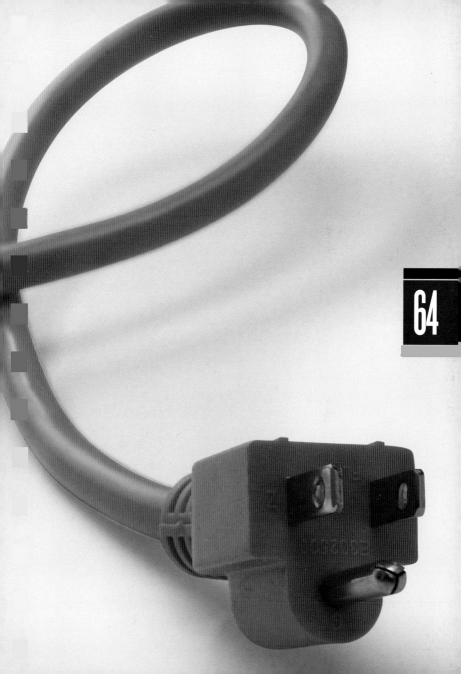

64

EXTENSION LADDER

Ranging in length from 16 to 40 feet in 2-foot increments, extension ladders put most projects safely within reach. To insure you don't buy a ladder that comes up short, the rule of thumb is to purchase one at least 7 feet taller than the height of the object you need to reach.

When using a ladder to get on a roof, you must extend the ladder 3 feet higher than the roof, which would be three full rungs. A fully extended 24-foot ladder leaning against a house, minus the 3-foot overlap, should be 21-feet high and the foot of the ladder should be planted 5 $\frac{1}{2}$ feet from the wall, at a 75-degree angle.

Be aware of electrical lines; even fiberglass ladders conduct electricity. When moving your ladder into position, plan your route beforehand. Squat slightly and with your dominant hand, grab a lower rung, then reach up and grab a rung with your other to steady it. Watch the lower part of the ladder as you walk; it will tell you if you're tilting and let you keep an eye on where you're walking.

Clearly marked on every ladder sold today are their weight limits. And when you're on top, don't reach out to the side. If your belt buckle extends past the ladder rail, you're overreaching. When working with tools, OSHA (Occupational Safety and Health Administration) recommends using a hand line attached to a bucket and that you pull your tools up once you are in a safe working position.

JUXTAPOSITION *Do you need both a stepladder and an extension ladder? Consider Werner's Telescoping Folding Ladder (pictured). It converts into a scaffold as well, and features configurations for stairwells.*

65

FLASHLIGHT

Working one-handed with a flashlight, or worse yet, with a light clamped between your teeth, is no way to operate. A spelunker's headlamp might be worth getting used to, or there's a variety of stationary lights with magnetic handles or movable necks to make aiming and working easier.

We buy flashlights for one reason, and that's to illuminate a dark space. So lumens, a measure of brightness, matters. The more lumens a flashlight boasts, the brighter and farther the light will shine. Some manufacturers still rate brightness in candlepower; one candlepower is equal to 12.57 lumens.

Bulb type matters in both longevity of the bulb and batteries. Incandescent and Xenon lights are battery eaters, since they use battery power to create heat and light, though Xenon lights do provide very bright light. LEDs, or light emitting diodes, last longest of the bulbs and are easiest on the batteries, but the quality of light isn't as good as Xenon bulbs. Some LEDs produce clean white light, but many are tinted.

Casing material may be important, depending on the type of work you're doing. If camping, fishing, or plumbing is in your future, then a rugged aluminum body and water-resistant casing are certainly some things to consider. But if it's a just-in-case type of light to get you around during a power failure or what you reach for in the middle of the night when your wife gives you a nudge after having heard something, then a plastic body will do just fine.

66

NAIL SET

A nail set allows you to countersink nailheads without damaging the surrounding surface, then conceal the holes with wood filler. The nail set should fit the finishing nail's head so you can set the nail without making a hole larger than the nail head.

The head of a finishing nail has a slight concavity, and that's where to seat the nail set. Align the set with the shank of the nail, and using a 16-ounce hammer, strike the set until you've sunk the nail about $\frac{1}{8}$ inch below the wood's surface. One or two whacks ought to do it. Hard cap nail sets have a large plastic striking surface and an easy-to-grip shank, making it an easier tool to use.

Nail sets are handy if you use a nail gun, too. Sometimes the nail gun doesn't countersink the fastener. You can sink a pneumatic nail the same way you sink an old-fashioned finishing nail, but with the pneumatic kind, you won't find an easy to seat dimple to help you out. Instead, you'll have to balance the set on the nail's head and tap it.

FIT FOR THE JOB *While you can use a set that's one size larger than you need, don't try to use an undersize one—this can damage the tools cup-shaped tip. To ensure you've got the right size, get a set of four: $\frac{1}{32}$-, $\frac{1}{16}$-, $\frac{3}{32}$-, and $\frac{1}{8}$-inch.*

67

PAINTBRUSH/ROLLER

The last thing most of us want to do after prepping and painting a room is the necessary cleanup, but this will preserve your brushes and rollers for future use. Begin by removing the excess latex paint by scraping the brush, then rinse in lukewarm water with the bristles facing down. Dip the brush in a bucket of soapy water and agitate the brush, making sure not to bend the bristles against the bottom. Repeat this process as necessary, changing the water each time. If there's any dried paint in the brush, use a stiff nylon cleaning brush and comb the dried paint free.

When the brush is clean, wrap the bristles in a paper towel. The paper towel will wick away a lot of the water, and as the paper towel dries, it shrinks and helps keep the shape of the brush. You should never lean a drying brush on the bristles; it's kind of like going to bed with wet hair.

When selecting a roller cover, one thing you'll pay attention to is nap. Nap is the length of the cover's fibers. On a smooth wall, you'll use a shorter-napped roller cover like a 1/4-inch to 3/8-inch nap, and for stucco or brick, a longer nap will do the job, say a 3/4- to 1-inch nap. A cardboard roller core won't last very long, since it will absorb the moisture and lose its roundness. A plastic core not only holds its shape but also won't disintegrate after several jobs.

To clean a roller, use the arched edge of a 5-in-1 painter's tool to scrape as much paint from it as you can. Then run it under lukewarm water using the 5-in-1 as a squeegee until the paint is removed. Stand it on end, placing it on a folded paper towel, and let dry.

68

PICK

A pick is like a pipe wrench—not very versatile, but when you need it, nothing else works nearly as well. If you spend most of your time breaking up hard, rocky soil, get a railroad pick— the type with either two pointed ends or a narrow chisel tip on one side and a pick on the other. Although using a railroad pick to break soft and medium-hard rock has become a dying art, it can be done if there's a crack in the rock where you can drive in the tip of the pick.

The tool can also be used for chopping through asphalt, and it's effective at severing small roots when equipped with a pick blade on one end and a mattock on the other. The mattock is the wide curved side, and, like any digging tool, if it's dinged or the metal appears dull, break out that file and hone the edge. You'll be glad you did.

PICKING THE BEST *Figuring out which to add to your arsenal? Select one with a drop-forged head. The head is balanced with the opposing pick or mattock and usually weighs 5 to 6 pounds. A pick isn't very heavy, but what makes it so effective is momentum. The weight of the swiftly swung head combined with a compact striking surface makes it an extremely effective digging tool. The angle of the head aids in both digging and prying, but it isn't the only thing providing leverage: a strong 36-inch handle made of hickory or fiberglass is instrumental in this tool's overall strength.*

69

PLUMBER'S SNAKE

When the old plunger just isn't cutting it, try a plumber's snake, sometimes called a hand auger, to unclog your drains. This hand-cranked drain-clearing tool has a long flexible steel cable that's extremely effective at clearing obstructions from tubs, showers, sinks, toilets, and drain lines.

Snakes come in a variety of sizes and lengths. For most people, a 3/8-inch-diameter, 20-foot-long snake is all you'll ever need. At the business end of the snake is a spring-shaped head wider than the snake itself. This "spring," really, engages the clog, and as the snake gets rotated and pulled and pushed, it breaks up the clog. Once the snake engages the clog, it will be more difficult to turn the snake. Push into the clog and pull back, but don't force the snake; there's a chance it can get stuck or snap off.

If it's a sink drain you're clearing, make sure there's some water in it. Not only will this provide some much needed lubrication, but also the water pressure along with the snake might send the clog exactly where you want it—down the drain and gone.

BACKED UP *If your kitchen drain clogs regularly, make sure your dishwashing habits are not contributing to the problem. The worst kitchen drain clogger is grease. We suggest pouring off grease from cookware into a container, then disposing of it when it has cooled. Also, remove and inspect the trap to confirm that hardened minerals or debris is not blocking it. Replace the trap if its internal diameter had been reduced by hardened buildup. And then it's time to take out your plumber's snake to thoroughly clear those pipes!*

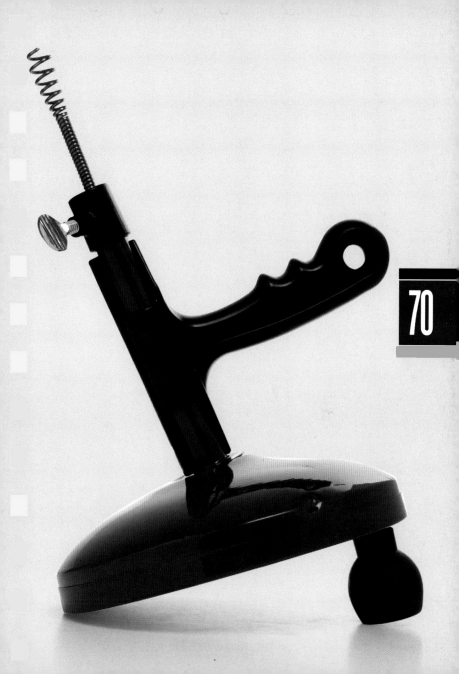

70

POCKET HOLE JIG

A pocket hole jig is a tool for making quick, strong joints in wood. Whether you're a weekend warrior or bona fide artisan woodworker, this tool will not only help you get great results when building cabinets, bookcases, entertainment centers, and the like, but also deliver these results almost immediately.

A pocket hole jig allows you to drill a hole at a very shallow angle into a piece of wood. A screw is then driven through this hole and into an adjoining piece of wood to create a tight, strong joint. Because the hole is drilled on a shallow angle, the screw won't protrude out the other board and a significant amount of the screw's threading is centered on the joint. It's fast and strong, and you don't have to wait around for the glue to dry.

The jig is one part of the equation; the other is a stepped drill bit. A stepped drill bit does two jobs simultaneously. First, it bores a hole large enough to accommodate the screw head. Then, because it's stepped, the thinner tip bores a pilot hole for the screw to follow, so it won't split your workpiece. Prices range from $6 for an entry level model (remember, you get what you pay for) to $100 for something more suited to a professional.

ELECTRIC JIG WONDER *For the dedicated carpenter with money to burn, there's the Kreg line of electric and pneumatic power tools, sure to give you a perfect pocket hole each and every time. Some of these models are much pricier than the handheld options (one which performs five pocket holes at once is close to five digits), but working with an automatic jig can be a real time saver.*

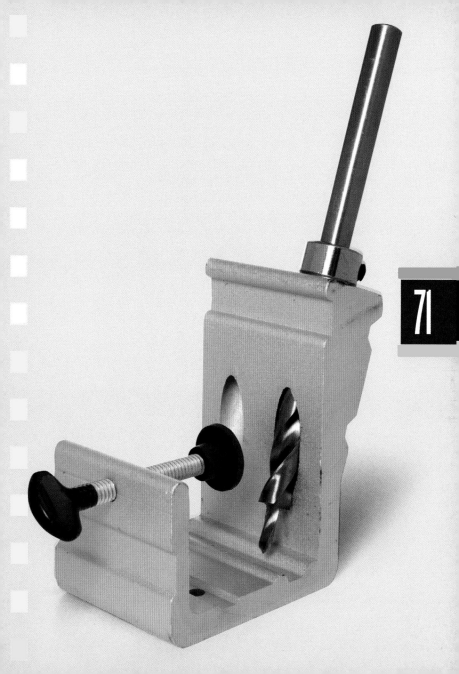

71

POST-HOLE DIGGER

No matter how you look at it, using a post-hole digger is serious work. Squeeze the handles together, drive it into the ground, separate the handles so the scoops grab up some dirt, remove dirt, and repeat. It's a tough slog, especially if the ground is hard.

When you're digging in hard soil or clay, loosen the dirt with a good-sized digging bar. Once you've got a good amount loosened, use the post-hole digger to remove the loosened soil. To get around roots or rocks, rotate the blades so you can get around the interference. When digging a post hole, it's best to start with a narrow hole and dig wider as you get deeper. This will make a more stable footing for your posts.

Extremely loose or dry soil is another challenge. The soil needs to be moist, otherwise you won't be able to remove it with a post-hole digger, as the clamping action of the jaws is not effective on these materials. You must be able to compact the soil you're removing.

A dull cutting edge will make this job tougher than it has to be, so you might want to dance a file over the cutting edges, tuning them up just a bit.

For a couple of holes, this tool is very useful. But if you've got a long fencing project or a deck with a dozen footings to dig, forgo this tool and head off to your local rental center to rent an auger. You'll be happy you did.

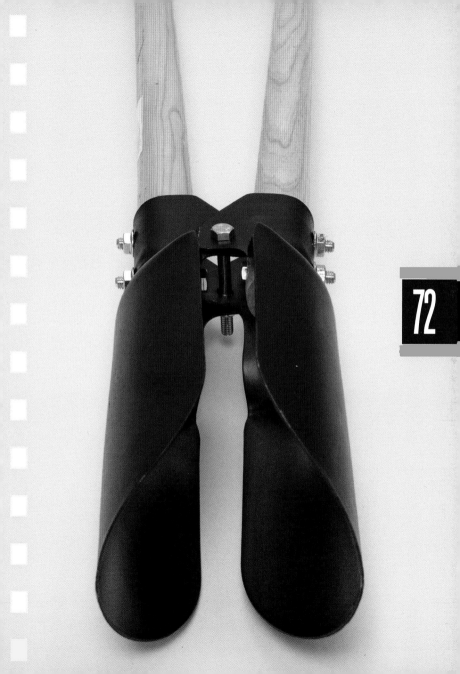

72

SAFETY GLASSES

Safety glasses are the single most important tool you'll ever own. You all know the old saying "It's all fun and games until someone loses an eye." Well, don't let anything get in the way of a good old time, then.

We're not talking about those goofy goggles we had to wear in high school that looked like a scuba diver's mask. We mean stylish glasses that could probably replace your favorite sunglasses.

Many manufacturers offer glasses with adjustable rubberized frames for maximum comfort. While comfort is important, it is recommended that the glasses provide maximum coverage and are made from high-impact plastic. But that's not all the protection you'll need, since you'll wear these indoors and out: glare reduction is also a must. Smoke-tinted or mirrored lenses will certainly reduce the risk of sun-blindness, but make sure your glasses also meet the stringent ANSI Z87.1-2003 UV protection ratings. While you're at it, get antifog lenses too. Let nothing interrupt your view, especially when you've got a power tool with a razor-sharp bit spinning at 10,000 rpm in your hands.

Switching back and forth between prescription glasses and safety glasses can be a huge pain. The only thing worse is saddling a set of safety goggles over your prescription glasses. But you don't have to sweat it anymore. For the ultimate tool kit, invest in a pair of prescription safety glasses, so you can focus on other things.

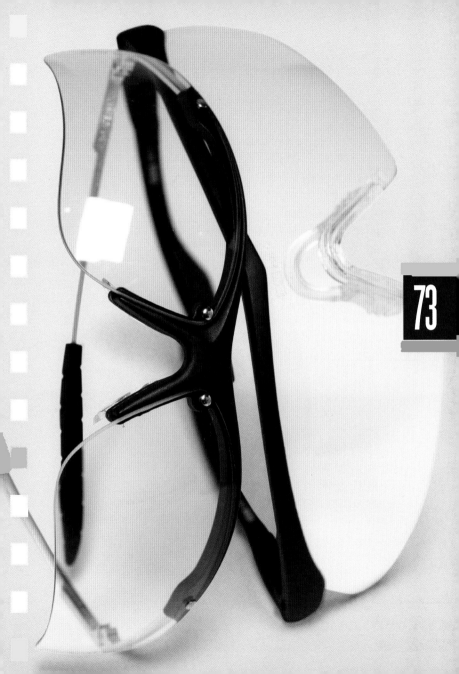

73

SOLDERING TORCH

Whether you're sweating pipes, making jewelry, or creating a crème brûlée in the kitchen, a soldering torch is your go-to. Look for a self-lighting option like Turbo Torch. This swirl combustion concentrates the flame's heat, reducing brazing time and saving gas. For jewelry and lamp making, you'll need a number of nozzles for directing the flame from a pinpoint to a wider warming flame. For sweating pipes, one good nozzle is all you really need.

Sweating a pipe is a lot like house painting: it's all about the prep. Once the pipe is cut to length using a tube cutter, clean the pipe ends and remove the burrs and any oxidation. Use a clean piece of sandpaper on the outside and a stiff wire brush on the inside.

Brush some plumbing flux on the abraded surfaces and assemble the joint. Fire up the torch and move the flame around the joint to heat it evenly. When sweating a copper pipe, it will first get shiny as the flux melts, but then it will dull. When this happens, apply the solder: move the flame away from the joint and not near anything combustible, and apply the lead-free solder to the joint. The solder will wick in and you should have a smooth run of solder surrounding the joint. While the pipe is still warm, apply some flux and wipe the joint thoroughly with a clean rag.

Lead-free solder is used for water supply lines, but it isn't your only choice. Tin/lead solders are also called soft solders. The higher the tin content, the greater the tensile and shear strength of the joint. When there's a higher lead content, the joint cools more slowly and the solder can be worked into the joint for a smoother appearance.

74

VOLT/OHMMETER

While water seeks to fill space, electricity searches for a conductor. You're able to see when a faucet isn't delivering water or when a drain drains slowly—but it's simply not possible to see where electricity is flowing. That's why it's crucial to have a volt/ohmmeter in your toolbox.

This tool is far more versatile than its two-part name suggests. Aside from measuring voltage and resistance (ohms), it also measures current flow (amperage), and most modern versions emit a tone to indicate a complete circuit (continuity).

There are two types of multimeters. An analog meter is generally less expensive and has a pointer that moves across a printed scale to indicate ohms, amperage, continuity, and so on. However, its functionality is limited by the width of the scale's pointer and its range. Accuracy can also be problematic, compromised by vibrations, precision printing on the labels, the lack of calibrations, and errors introduced because of non-horizontal use of the mechanical display. Analog volt/ohmmeters typically measure within 3% accuracy, which may not be precise enough for your needs—certainly not if you're trying to diagnose electrical problems in your car by tracing voltage drops.

We recommend purchasing a more expensive digital meter, which will run you a few hundred dollars, and will reliably provide you with a digital readout accurate to 0.5% on the DC voltage ranges. It's unlikely you'll need a Category IV meter (used to measure house meters), so look for a Category III if you'll be testing appliance outlets or distribution panels. Always check your meter's specific measuring range before using it.

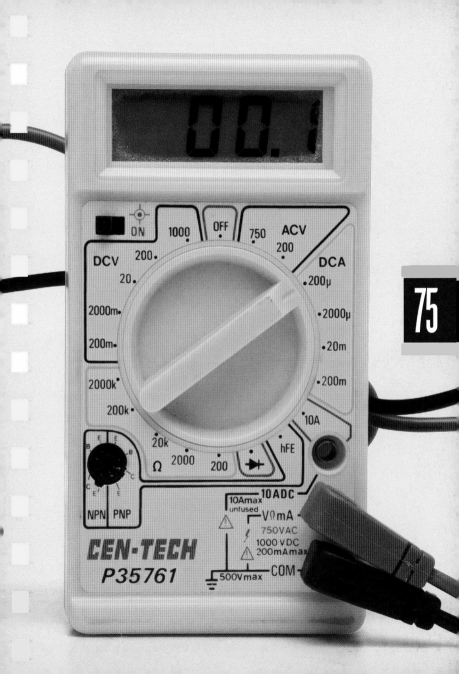

INDEX

PHOTOGRAPHY CREDITS

All photography by Chad Hunt, with the following exceptions:

Zach DeSart: 4

Anja Hitzenberger: 143

iStockphoto: 87, 140-141; Ken Davidson: 81; Craig Hill: 70-71; Günter Jurczik: 88-89; John Verner: 12-13

Martin Poole: 7

Ben Stechschulte/Redux: 61

Studio D: Philip Friedman: 52-53

Book design by Jon Chaiet

Library of Congress Cataloging-in-Publication Data
Kidd, James, 1963-
  75 tools every man needs, and how to use them like a pro / text by James Kidd ; photography by Chad Hunt.
     p. cm.
  At head of title: Popular mechanics.
  Includes index.
  ISBN 978-1-58816-872-6
  1. Tools. I. Popular mechanics (Chicago, Ill. : 1959) II. Title. III. Title: Seventy-five tools every man needs, and how to use them like a pro.
  TJ1195.K53 2011
  621.9--dc22

                    2010034483

10 9 8 7 6 5 4 3 2 1

Published by Hearst Books
A division of Sterling Publishing Co., Inc.
387 Park Avenue South, New York, NY 10016

Popular Mechanics is a registered trademark of Hearst Communications, Inc.

www.popularmechanics.com

For information about custom editions, special sales, premium and corporate purchases, please contact Sterling Special Sales Department at 800-805-5489 or specialsales@sterlingpublishing.com.

Distributed in Canada by Sterling Publishing
c/o Canadian Manda Group, 165 Dufferin Street
Toronto, Ontario, Canada M6K 3H6

Distributed in Australia by Capricorn Link (Australia) Pty. Ltd.
P.O. Box 704, Windsor, NSW 2756 Australia

Manufactured in China

Sterling ISBN 978-1-58816-872-6

Popular Mechanics

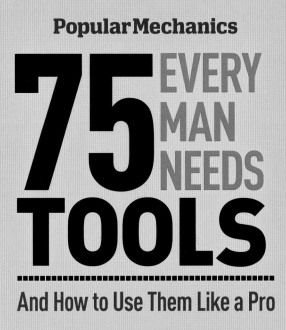

75 EVERY MAN NEEDS TOOLS

And How to Use Them Like a Pro

Text by James Kidd • Photography by Chad Hunt
Produced by Michele Ervin

HEARST BOOKS
A division of Sterling Publishing Co., Inc.

New York / London
www.sterlingpublishing.com